The Dealer *is dedicated to our dads.*

Rex Burnett, a great dad, loving husband,
and the best hot-rod cutaway artist of all time.

James J. Ciardella, a loving father,
devoted partner to mom, and a storyteller.

They gave us their passion, knowing it would live forever in our hearts.

THE DEALER

*How One California Dealership Fueled
the Rise of Ferrari Cars in America*

JIM CIARDELLA

Prometheus Books
Guilford, Connecticut

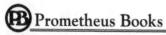

Prometheus Books

An imprint of Globe Pequot, the trade division of
The Rowman & Littlefield Publishing Group, Inc.
4501 Forbes Blvd., Ste. 200
Lanham, MD 20706
www.rowman.com

Distributed by NATIONAL BOOK NETWORK

British Library Cataloguing in Publication Information available

Library of Congress Cataloging-in-Publication Data

Names: Ciardella, Jim, 1949– author.
Title: The dealer : how one California dealership fueled the rise of
    Ferrari cars in America / Jim Ciardella.
Description: Lanham, MD : Rowman & Littlefield, [2022] | Summary: "The
    Dealer is the story of how one dealership, the legendary Ferrari of Los
    Gatos, fueled the rise of the iconic Italian sports car in the U.S.
    market on its way to becoming the number-one Ferrari dealer in North
    America. Along the way, its founders made friends, enemies, and millions
    of dollars, only to lose everything in the blink of an eye"—Provided
    by publisher.
Identifiers: LCCN 2021054677 (print) | LCCN 2021054678 (ebook) | ISBN
    9781633887558 (cloth) | ISBN 9781633887565 (epub)
Subjects: LCSH: Ferrari of Los Gatos (Automobile dealer) | Automobile
    Dealers—California—Los Gatos. | Ferrari automobile—History. |
    Selling—Automobiles—California—Los Gatos. | Automobile industry and
    trade.
Classification: LCC HF5439.A8 C55 2022 (print) | LCC HF5439.A8 (ebook) |
    DDC 629.22209794/73—dc23/eng/20220112
LC record available at https://lccn.loc.gov/2021054677
LC ebook record available at https://lccn.loc.gov/2021054678

FOREWORD

MY NAME IS ROY BRIZIO. I STARTED GOING TO DRAG CAR RACES WITH my dad Andy when I was five years old. He was the flagman at the Half Moon Bay drag strip. When I grew up, I worked for him at the Champion Speed Shop in South San Francisco

I knew what I wanted to do early in life. When I decided to start my own business, my dad said, "You don't want to do this, Roy; you won't make any money." He thought I should keep working at Champion Speed Shop, where I got a steady paycheck. But I was a young kid in my 20s with a dream, and I wanted my own shop.

For a long time, I thought he might have been right. I opened Roy Brizio Street Rods in the late 1970s and struggled for probably 20 years, working six or seven days a week. But I always believed that if you do something from your heart and you love to do it, eventually you'll make some money along the way.

One of the reasons I survived and succeeded was a phone call I received in 1978 from a Ferrari dealer asking me to build a hot rod for him. I couldn't believe this guy trusted me. He was a successful Ferrari dealer on top of the world, and I was just getting started. Brian Burnett not only gave me one of my first jobs but also helped me gain recognition when nobody knew too much about me. For more than 40 years, we've been friends, and I've built many cars for him.

When his dealership, Ferrari of Los Gatos, was rolling, he'd say, "Let's build these cars." And when he wasn't rolling, we didn't do anything. As soon as he was okay again, he'd say, "Let's build a car." He was always good to me.

Building cars for Brian and getting to know him was exciting. I remember he was so successful not only with the dealership but also with his family. He had a beautiful wife, great-looking kids, and a beautiful home in Los Gatos. I went to his house for a party, and what I remember the most was a movie screen that dropped out of the ceiling. I'd never seen anything like that before. I remember thinking, *Oh my God, Brian has it all*.

The dealership he built was second to none. There were so many cars on the lot: beautiful new Ferraris along with classic older Ferraris, hot rods, muscle cars, and other hard-to-find models. I'd visit and just dream of having something like that one day.

The showroom was small with only a few cars in it. Most people would stand at the window and drool. New Ferraris were sitting out front with just a little chain between them and the street. It was something you would never do today. While the staff at most other dealerships wore suits and ties, the team at Ferrari of Los Gatos wore jeans and a polo shirt. Even at the height of his success, Brian wore jeans, a Ralph Lauren polo shirt, and blue surfer tennis shoes. I don't think I've ever seen him dressed in anything else.

I'm proud to have built a couple of award-winning hot rods with Ferrari engines in them. However, it would never have happened if Brian hadn't built the Deucari, a 1932 Ford Roadster with a Ferrari V-12 engine that won the 1979 America's Most Beautiful Roadster (AMBR) award at the Grand National Roadster Show in Oakland, California. That was a huge deal at the time. No one would ever have done that if it wasn't for Brian. After that, hot rod guys would come to me and say, "I want a Ferrari motor in my car like the one Brian Burnett did." Brian loved Ferraris, but I think he loved hot rods just as much. I saw him get more excited about an old Ford than a brand-new Ferrari.

I'm glad that author Jim Ciardella took the time and energy to highlight Brian's passion for cars and show how he built Ferrari of Los Gatos into an iconic dealership. He spent many years recording Brian's story and interviewing people associated with him. His book, *The Dealer: How One California Dealership Fueled the Rise of Ferrari Cars in America*, highlights many hard-to-believe stories of what happened there. My connection is a small part of the story. The book tells how the dealership rose to the top, only to be gobbled up by Ferrari along with other dealers.

Contents

I credit Brian, and I sincerely mean this, with giving me a chance and letting me build some great cars for him. I was a young guy, and he trusted me to do this. Like Brian (or anyone else), people walk into your life for different reasons. Some of them stay in your life forever, and others are in and out within a year or two. I've been lucky to stay friends with almost all my customers, and Brian has remained a friend to this day. In fact, he just helped me find a 1955 model car that a customer wanted to turn into a hot rod. I'm not sure anyone else could have found one as quick and in such good shape. That was something Ferrari of Los Gatos was well known for. If they couldn't find a car for you, chances are that no one could.

Thanks, Brian, it's been a heck of a ride.

Roy Brizio
December 2021

PREFACE

LOS GATOS, CALIFORNIA, WAS THE HOME OF A FERRARI DEALERSHIP. AS a kid, that's all I knew about that little town. I grew up in Palo Alto, about 45 minutes north. And the thought of a Ferrari made me shiver with excitement. Seeing or hearing one would stop me from whatever I was doing to watch the magnificent car. If you are a Ferrari enthusiast, maybe you can relate.

I moved to Los Gatos and met Brian Burnett, owner of Ferrari of Los Gatos, about 10 years after it closed. I told him of my lifetime love of Ferraris and how I'd always wanted one. The next words out of his mouth were, "Do you still want one?"

I said yes, and he continued, "I know about an '82 308 GTSi, red on tan, with just 12,000 miles. And it's had only one owner." The next day, I bought the car and started my friendship with Brian. He never stopped telling me stories about the Ferrari dealership and finished each tale with, "Someone ought to write a book about it." One night, after many stories and his predictable conclusion, I told him, "I'll do it. I'll write the book."

How difficult could it be? I thought. I had met a guy with incredible stories about the car I loved. There must be a reason for that chance encounter, I reasoned.

Since the night we decided to tell the story of what really happened at Ferrari of Los Gatos, we've spent thousands of hours writing *The Dealer: How One California Dealership Fueled the Rise of Ferrari Cars in America*. In the process, Brian's passion about his 20-year ride rubbed off on me. I finished every interview amazed with what I'd heard and couldn't wait to get my thoughts down on paper. Other individuals shared their experiences, and I've weaved their accounts into the book as well. The stories I heard were so exciting that they made it easy to find time to write about how Ferrari of Los Gatos touched so many lives.

Even as I write this short preface, there's an adrenaline rush to share the tale. It's the story of how a couple of 30-year-olds, on a tiny corner lot of a small town, built the largest Ferrari dealership in America. They succeeded by doing things differently than the other dealerships, and people liked it. But when Enzo Ferrari died, we lost more than a man: we lost his passion, and things changed. His successors felt that the dealers Enzo credited for building a profitable market in North America were not important anymore. Brian was determined to prove them wrong.

Along with Ferraris, Brian built and sold hot rods, muscle cars, and other classic cars, and the dealership got a reputation for being able to find any car. And Brian was the first person to ever put a Ferrari engine in a hot rod.

Over the years, the lore and legend of Ferrari of Los Gatos has been told and retold by car enthusiasts around the world. I'm pleased to share these stories and other great memories from the days of Ferrari of Los Gatos along with Brian's personal life and his behind-the-scenes experiences with Ferrari.

What happened on the corner of Pageant Way and East Main Street may never happen again, but the memory of what took place there will be remembered forever by the people who lived the story.

I hope you enjoy the ride.

Jim Ciardella
December 2021

Introduction

In Silicon Valley, most start-ups are considered a success when they become profitable. In 1976, Ferrari of Los Gatos made a profit of $31,000 in its first month. This was quite a feat considering its founders, Richard Rivoir and Brian Burnett, had started with only $20,000.

By using a rogue approach to sell Ferraris, doing what no other dealer would dare, and fueled by the unwavering belief they could not fail, Brian and Richard sold more Ferraris on a small corner in Los Gatos, California, than anyone else in the world.

Enzo Ferrari's marketing mavens had advised him that America might be the wrong market to pursue. Americans, they insisted, didn't understand the value of the car and, therefore, would never pay the price. But Brian had a different vision, one he dreamed about as a 12-year-old boy. Twenty years later, his dream would come true when Ferrari of Los Gatos opened its doors, put owning a Ferrari within reach of the average American, and created a profitable market for Ferrari cars in North America.

But this story isn't just about business—it's also about the people who lived the dream daily. It includes a cast of characters and unusual situations that are, at times, hard to believe, like Rueben, who picked up and delivered cars for Ferrari of Los Gatos for 15 years. "I'd just dropped off a car and received payment in a briefcase loaded with cash—$185,000. I took a taxi to my next stop and picked up a Ferrari Mondial Cabriolet to take back to Los Gatos. On the drive home, I stopped at a gas station and ended up having to outrun thieves who were after the money. Thank God Ferraris are fast."

The assortment of new Ferraris and other classic cars, seldom seen on other dealer lots, attracted visitors from around the world. As a result,

Ferrari of Los Gatos became well known across America and throughout the world as well. If you worked there, your business card held the status of a black American Express card. It could usher you into the best restaurants without a reservation and the most exclusive nightclubs without having to stand in line, and it worked in Scottsdale or Miami as well as it did in Los Gatos.

Many customers were celebrities. One Major League Baseball player picked up his car but couldn't drive it home. He'd purchased the car without realizing it had a manual transmission. He may have been a great baseball player, but driving a stick shift was not part of his skill set.

Then there's the well-known movie star who turned a routine delivery to her Beverly Hills home into a kidnapping. And there was the time Brian located a hard-to-find Ferrari F40 for a world-famous rock star, earning not only a nice profit but front-row seats at a sold-out concert. But the most infamous customers may have been the ones who paid cash and refused to have their names on any paperwork.

The dealership lived through the well-known ups and downs of the automobile industry and took Brian on a journey into the world of Ferrari only few have ever seen. His tell-it-like-it-is personality and unique selling style turned Ferrari of Los Gatos into the number one dealer. He reached sales of almost $50 million one year ($136 million in 2021 dollars) at a time when new Ferraris sold for $50,000 to $80,000 and used Ferraris averaged $15,000 to $45,000. Along the way, he made friends, enemies, and millions of dollars, only to lose everything in the blink of an eye.

For when Enzo died, things changed, unfortunately. The new regime at Ferrari had a different plan. Rather than cherishing the exquisite racing machine, racing fell out of favor, and a Ferrari became a mere product to be sold with the highest possible profit. Ferrari developed a plan to restructure the way their cars would be sold in North America that sidelined innovative dealers who were in it for the love of the car. Ultimately, that plan replaced honor and respect with greed and ego, destroying many dealers' lives.

Something magical took place on the corner of Pageant Way and East Main Street in Los Gatos, and although it wasn't sustainable after Enzo's death, it still lives on in the memories of those it touched.

CHAPTER ONE

Brian's Long Ride

(1995)

HE HEARD THE ROAR OF THE 12-CYLINDER ENGINE, AND HIS DAD'S voice echoed in his mind. *"Hello, Brian. Here's the Ferrari you asked us to pick up. It was a long ride, but your mother and I made it. She sure is a beauty. Your mother, not the car."*

Glancing over his shoulder, Brian Burnett realized there was no car at the curb and that his parents had moved north years ago. But he could still hear his mom laughing at her husband's flirtatious remark.

It seemed like yesterday—not 20 years—since Bill Harrah's Modern Classic Motors approved a Ferrari dealership to be located on the corner of Pageant Way and East Main Street in Los Gatos, California.

Twenty years?

Looking through the glass showroom window at the cars he loved, Brian turned the key to lock the dealership door.

Memories rushed through his mind. He thought about the drawings that made his dad, Rex Burnett, the most recognized hot-rod cutaway artist in the world. *It seems like I was just downstairs in the basement watching him sketch.* Brian wondered if his dad had taught him everything, or were there more fenders, bumpers, and hood ornaments he should know about? And he remembered watching the race with his dad on an air force runway in 1954. Jim Kimberly won in the red number 5 Ferrari. He could still hear his engine fire up. *What a sound that was!* The thought brought a smile to his face.

It seemed like his entire life had revolved around fast cars in general and Ferraris in particular. What now, what next? What could ever take the place of a business that allowed him to sell those exclusive, fast, and exciting cars? *"I'd had Camelot for 20 years, minus the happily-ever-aftering part."*

He recalled Enzo Ferrari smiling at a picture of the Deucari, a '32 Ford deuce roadster Brian had built with a Ferrari V-12 engine. "You did this?" Enzo had asked. When Brian nodded, Enzo shook his hand, confirming approval. What could replace selling cars for Enzo, the man who turned a childhood dream into the world's greatest automobile dynasty?

Brian's mind was racing as fast as the cars he sold. There were so many stories to remember, people he'd met, and lives changed during his years as the proud owner of Ferrari of Los Gatos.

And, of course, there was the sinister duo from Italy that took it all away. By halting the shipment of new cars from the factory, they had undermined the dealership and badmouthed Brian to be a no-good dealer incapable of adequately representing Ferrari. *Incapable?* He'd sold more Ferraris in those 20 years than anyone else on the planet.

The final click of the lock brought him back to the present moment. It was time to go. He realized that of all the lives affected by this dealership, the most transformed was his own.

He put the key in his pocket, turned around, and walked away from the street corner his business had shaped for two decades. As he crossed East Main Street, the noises, voices, and faces of the dealership seemed to follow him like ghosts—customers, bankers, employees, celebrities, dealers, and friends—and he thought about his wife, kids, and parents who'd supported him.

How did I lose all this?

Greed and dishonesty can destroy anything, even when you're number one. And he'd been number one, no doubt about it, for a long, long time.

Brian turned around to look back one more time at the place that had filled him with so much pride and knew that no matter what the future might hold, his time with Ferrari of Los Gatos had been the most incredible ride of his life.

CHAPTER TWO

Passion for the Car

(1954)

BRIAN AND HIS DAD ARRIVED AT THE RACE EARLY. YOUNG BRIAN sensed it would be exciting, but he had no clue that the day would change the rest of his life.

Brian's family had been all about cars for generations. His dad, Rex Burnett, grew up watching the automobile replace the horse and buggy and developed an art technique called a cutaway drawing. It showed a car from the inside out, illustrating what it looked like under its skin. It was introduced in the September 1948 issue of *Hot Rod* magazine as the "Rex Burnett Center Spread Hot-Rod Cutaway Drawing" and became a monthly feature.

His dad's passion for cars spilled over to his young son. Brian seemed interested in anything to do with cars. His dad noticed him staring at other vehicles when they were out for a ride and started pointing out roof slopes, fender and grille shapes, emblems, and badges to teach Brian how to identify a particular automobile. Family and friends would test young Brian by giving him a clue about a car and asking him, "What is it?" At four years old, he could usually tell them the year, make, and model. Rex watched with excitement and pride as his son amazed the rest of the family with his depth and breadth of knowledge.

It was Sunday, June 6, 1954. Brian and his dad were at the Sports Car Club of America (SCCA) race held at Chanute Air Force Base in Rantoul, Illinois. In 1948, the SCCA started public street road racing in Watkins Glen, New York, followed by similar races in Pebble Beach,

California, and Elkhart Lake, Wisconsin. Unfortunately, a tragedy occurred in 1952 when driver Fred Wacker struck onlookers sitting on a curb, killing a seven-year-old boy and injuring 10 others. The accident caused the end of street racing in the United States.

General Curtis Lemay, a sports car enthusiast and head of the U.S. Strategic Air Command, came to the rescue, turning U.S. Air Force base runways into weekend racetracks and saving SCCA racing events.

On this day, there would be no takeoffs or landings. Instead, airplanes were parked to the side so that shiny sports cars could fly around the runways. Dick Boyd, another SCCA racing enthusiast, had invited Brian and his dad to the race to thank Rex for drawing the Boyd Mecca custom sports car.

As VIP guests, Brian and his dad had passes to the pit area where the cars and crews awaited the start of the race. Of course, it was exciting to be close to those huge air force B-52 bombers, but for Brian, being close to the cars, drivers, and mechanics was even more exciting. Sure, he'd been close to cars at his dad's photo shoots and had spent countless

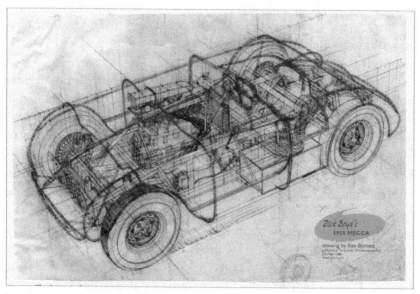

Rex Burnett cutaway drawing, 1954. *John Burnett Library*

4

hours going through pictures his dad had received from magazines, but that day, those pictures came to life.

Almost 50 years earlier, young Enzo Ferrari, like Brian, attended a car race with his father and brother in Bologna, Italy. He talked about that race his entire life and gave it partial credit for his extreme passion for fast cars. Enzo's cars not only carried his name but were built with his spirit as well. That spirit encircled Brian at the SCCA race that day since some of the cars he saw were Enzo's creations.

For Brian, walking around the pit area during that SCCA race was overwhelming. Being so close to the cars was a visceral experience—the smells, sounds, and sights—it was as if the place consumed his entire body. With eyes moving quickly, head turning side to side, and feet dancing, Brian watched as the drivers and mechanics readied for the race. And then he noticed Jim Kimberly, the previous year's SCCA champion, getting into car number 5, a red Ferrari 375 MM. Kimberly was easy to spot. He had a red car transporter, wore a red helmet, had a red driving suit with a button-down collar, had red driving gloves, and employed red-suited mechanics.

"What do you think son, shall we go sit down?" Brian's dad asked as other excited fans filled the bleachers. The hustle and bustle made Brian's heart beat fast. Trying to catch his breath, he turned to answer his father but couldn't. The roar of Jim Kimberly's V-12 engine firing up silenced everyone. All eyes turned in the direction of the deafening sound. For young Brian, the howl of that engine pierced his heart and soul and started a lifelong love affair with Ferraris.

The 1954 car racing season turned out to be the year Ferrari triumphed over the Cunningham sports car, king of the American racing scene for the prior three years. At MacDill Air Force Base in Tampa, Florida, Jim Kimberly brought his new 4.5 Ferrari 375 MM to the starting line. Despite having to race in the rain that day, Kimberly beat the seasoned Phil Walters, who drove a Cunningham with an engine 60 cubic inches larger than the Ferrari. And, to prove this was no fluke, Kimberly did it again at Hunter Air Force Base in Savannah, Georgia, beating Sherwood Johnston's Cunningham by an entire lap.

Jim Kimberly and his number 5 Ferrari 375 MM, circa 1954. Popular Science Magazine, *June 1955*

Kimberly had won six of seven races by the time the Chanute Air Force Base race took place, and it wasn't easy to find another car capable of mounting a challenge. Nevertheless, he ended up winning 16 of 17 events that season.

The competition included dozens of Jaguar XK120s, an Alfa Romeo 2.9, a Porsche, the Allard J-2, a 4.1 Ferrari, and a 2.9 Ferrari. So it's no wonder Brian fell in love with Kimberly's car.

On race day, a Porsche was the biggest challenge for the 4.5 Ferrari, that is, until the car spun out on the first lap. After that, Kimberly needed only a mile to prove the Ferrari's power and his driving ability. He passed two cars on the first bend and overtook an Allard to take the lead. After that, he kept the crowd entertained by going faster and faster, lap after lap, hitting a top speed of 148 mph.

The race turned out as predicted, with Kimberly putting on a spectacular show and finishing first ahead of a Jaguar driven by Loyal Katskee. The third- and fifth-place cars, driven by Eppie Lunken and Richard Lyeth, were the only other Ferraris in the race. Ferrari impressed the crowd that day, especially twelve-year-old Brian, who to this day says he can still hear the sound of Kimberly's engine starting up.

While Brian became hooked on cars early, his family had been making car history long before he was born.

In 1923, his grandmother had mounted a successful campaign to convince his grandfather, John Burnett, to move the family west. Her mother and four sisters had moved to Compton, California, three years earlier. Brian's grandfather first traveled there by train, purchased a grocery store with living quarters in the back, and returned to get the family. Heading west with his family, John planned on driving.

That plan had a couple of challenges.

First of all, there were no paved roads.

Henry Ford's low-priced, mass-produced Model T Ford had put the automobile within reach of many Americans, and that created the need for better roads. So, on November 23, 1921, President Warren G. Harding signed the Federal Highway Act and created the Bureau of Public Roads. The act also provided funding for a system to build paved two-lane interstate highways across the country. Still, in 1923, when Brian's grandfather began the trek to California, the government was just getting started.

The other challenge?

Brian's grandfather didn't have a car.

So, with no car and no roads, he hired a neighbor with a horse-drawn buggy to take the family down Boston Mountain to the Frisco train depot located about three miles from their home in Pettigrew, Arkansas. The Burnetts then boarded a small train that brought them to Fayetteville, Arkansas, where Grandfather John went to the local Ford dealership and bought a brand-new 1923 Model T open touring car. The car came equipped with Snap-On Isinglass curtains for severe weather, an extra spare tire and tube, and expandable running board luggage racks.

Brian's grandfather was a pioneer for sure. After buying the car, he turned to the salesman and said, "I don't know how to drive this thing." The salesman replied, "Don't worry, I'll teach you." And he did. They went on a four- or five-mile training drive, and at the end, the salesman told

Brian's grandfather he drove very well and would have no difficulty on the journey to California.

Most cars stayed in the cities because the lack of a paved highway system made long-distance travel treacherous. But that didn't stop Brian's grandfather. He was taking the family, his wife and five kids, on a trek to California, roads or not. His can-do attitude would show up in his grandson a couple of generations later.

Brian's grandfather crammed suitcases into the spaces between the fenders and hood and stowed camping equipment on the running board racks. Water bags hung from the crossbar that connected and stabilized the front fenders. There was enough room on the backseat for the older children, including Brian's father, to fit snugly, but the baby boy would have to ride on his mother's lap in the front passenger seat.

Early the following day, the seven Burnetts drove out of town toward Kansas. On the way, they'd wave to the construction crews using horse-drawn graders to build the first roads across America. The Kansas rain kept the Model T axle deep in mud, but a team of highway department horses always seemed to appear whenever the car got stuck. When they reached the Red River at Sayre, Oklahoma, they found no bridge to get to the other side. So instead, highway crews pulled cars across the sandy riverbed. Everyone had to keep their feet up and hold their suitcases on their laps as they crossed the river and water ran over the floorboards. The water splashed into the engine compartment as well. Once on the other side of the river, Brian's grandfather couldn't get the car started. He had to remove a wet coil and distributor cap from the engine, place them on a stick, and hold them over the small fire he'd built. He had to get them dry before they'd work again, but he also had to make sure not to burn or melt them. Once the parts were dry, he replaced them in the engine, restarted the car, and got back on the road. Talk about a pioneer. His effort to keep the car running makes today's regular maintenance seem a little less annoying.

Heavy rainstorms on the prairie continued making them stop by the side of the road or seek shelter regularly. Without a highway system to keep travelers on the same route, roadside restaurants and motels did not exist. Late every evening, they'd try to find a farmhouse where they could get something to eat and stay overnight. Prairie folks were usually welcoming and seemed to enjoy travelers who dropped in, especially when they drove up in a new car.

After checking out the car and asking a few questions, the farmer would provide a chicken dinner, a comfortable bed for Brian's grandparents, and pallets on the floor for the five children. In the morning, the woman of the house would serve a breakfast of home-cured ham, eggs, and biscuits, smothered in ham gravy. At departure time, Brian's grandfather would always thank the hosts and offer to pay something for their hospitality. Most farmers replied with something like, "Oh, t'warn't nothing much, but if you insist, would a quarter apiece be alright?"

It took more than three weeks to get to California from Arkansas (the same trip today takes about 37 hours). It was a challenging ride—and in a way for naught because the family didn't stay for long. Brian's great grandfather was in poor health, and Brian's grandfather was deluged with letters from brothers and sisters urging him to come home. So after less than six months out west, Brian's grandfather sold the grocery store and property in California and moved the family back to Pettigrew. Brian's dad, Rex, remembered little of the few months in California but did say, "It was probably the beginning of my love affair with the Golden State." He'd return with his family 39 years later, and 17-year-old Brian would attend Los Gatos High School.

Rex's family lived on the main road where log wagons, laden with virgin hardwoods, sometimes pressed so close to their house that they scraped the back porch as the teamsters "straightened" on the bend starting down Boston Mountain to the railhead at Pettigrew. In those days, roads in the Ozark Mountains were not only unpaved but also ungraded, and the ruts made by the countless horse and mule-drawn wagons and occasional passenger "buggy" defined the road.

As a young boy, Rex studied the tire tracks left by the rare Model T cars in the dusty road. Paper was hard to come by, so his detailed drawings of the impressions ended up on the cardboard boxes behind his father's grocery store. His love for automobiles and drawing constantly honed his natural talent as he filled the open spaces of his schoolbooks with car sketches. As a teenager, he studied the automotive ads in the *Saturday Evening Post* and *Collier's* magazine.

He seemed to have a front-row seat as Henry Ford's new industry was born and the automobile came to life. In the 1930s, when Ford's Model T cars cost $5, they got modified and renamed "cut-down, hop-ups," precursor to the name "hot rod."

While Rex continued sketching cars whenever he had a chance, the extent of his formal art training was limited to a beginner still-life class at Oklahoma State University. He joined the navy during World War II and continued to draw cars. Rex used his drawings to barter with other sailors, bringing him extra privileges or relieving him of unpleasant tasks. When the war ended, he decided to make California his home, get married, and start a family. He worked for the Douglas Aircraft Company and Lockheed Aircraft Corporation as a technical artist. There, he met Gary Davis, who was marketing a three-wheeled car called the Davis Divan. Davis needed someone to conceive and draw a body style for it—Rex got the job.

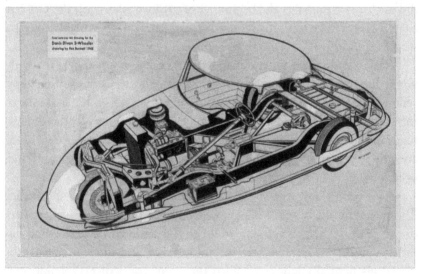

One of the first cutaway drawings by Rex Burnett, 1948. *John Burnett Library*

Through the Davis Divan project, he met Robert E. Petersen, who had just launched *Hot Rod* magazine. In September 1948, *Hot Rod* ran a feature article on the Davis Divan, including Rex's drawing, and the "Rex Burnett Center Spread Hot-Rod Cutaway Drawing" was born. He conceived the idea of enhancing the developing "hot rod" mania with a drawing style that suggested form and structure. Petersen liked what he saw and asked Rex to produce regular contributions in the "Hot Rod of the Month" section. While still working full-time, Rex created art for *Hot Rod* as well as *Motor Trend*, *Auto*, and *Cycle* magazines. Today, Rex Burnett is recognized internationally as the pioneer of cutaway drawings.

In 1952, Lockheed transferred Rex to Marietta, Georgia, ending the *Hot Rod* cutaway drawings. The magazine just didn't pay enough for Brian's dad to continue the time-consuming work. To supplement his income, he opened three Dog n Suds hot dog and root beer drive-in restaurants in the late 1950s. After school, Brian worked at one as a carhop. Not only did it give him some extra spending money, but it also provided an up-close look at the coolest cars in town.

One day, a newspaper ad caught Brian's attention. He'd been talking to his dad about needing transportation to work, and the thought of a motorcycle was exciting. Well, not just any motorcycle. The ad was for a Vincent Black Shadow, the English bike that held the land speed record of 138 mph. He'd always wanted to be the fastest on the road and knew the Vincent could outrun anything.

"I cut out the ad, showed it to my dad, and begged him to let me buy it. I'd saved up my own money, so he couldn't object to that, but no matter what I tried, he kept saying no. So finally, after many failed attempts, I asked him if we could just go look at it."

"We can go look at it, but you're not gonna buy it."

His dad loved classic cars and anything fast. So Brian was sure that once his dad saw the Vincent, he'd be bringing it home. After all, it was the world's fastest production motorcycle.

Sure enough, that night, it was sitting in their garage, and Brian had his transportation to work.

The Dog n Suds was an opportunity for Brian to meet people, talk to them about their cars, and, occasionally, challenge them to a road race.

1950 Vincent Black Shadow motorcycle. *Public domain photo, Wikimedia.org*

"It was amazing how many people thought their cars could outrun a motorcycle. They never had a chance. I left them in the dust every time." After experiencing the power and speed of Jim Kimberly's Ferrari at the SCCA race a few years earlier, Brian was fixated on speed—and winning, a goal that drove him forward in anything he did.

In 1959, Brian's dad received an offer he couldn't refuse. The Lockheed Aircraft Company had some special projects in California and needed skilled artists and designers. Lockheed offered to pay for relocating the family and two jobs, one for himself and one for his wife.

Rex had never forgotten his childhood Model T cross-country trip to California. So when Lockheed lured him to Sunnyvale, California, it didn't take long for him to pack up the family and move. They settled in Saratoga, a town neighboring Los Gatos.

Saratoga's only high school stopped at the 11th grade. Seventeen-year-old Brian was in the 12th grade and had to attend Los Gatos

High School. "It was fun going to high school in Los Gatos, especially because the girls thought my Georgia accent was cool."

Brian liked to hang out with school buddies in the Los Gatos library parking lot next to the high school. It turned out to be the first place he used his knowledge of cars to sell one. Wanting a different vehicle, Brian parked his car there with a for-sale sign in the window. Finding a willing buyer, he wondered if this might be a way to make a little extra money. He'd find a car someone would be willing to sell, and then he'd find a friend who would buy it. He sold a few for cash and occasionally took some money and a trade-in. He liked taking trades because he could make extra money selling two cars instead of one.

Little did he know that 14 years later, he'd be selling the most popular cars in the world from the corner of Pageant Way and East Main Street, a block away from that library parking lot.

Like Enzo, Brian was hooked on cars early in his life. His father's passion rubbed off on him, and watching Ferraris race as a young boy set him up for a life chasing these cars. Who would have suspected that he'd meet Enzo one day, making his childhood dream come true?

CHAPTER THREE

Persistence and a Dream

(1975)

RICHARD RIVOIR WORKED IN REAL ESTATE DEVELOPMENT BUT ALSO had a love for classic cars. He operated California Imports, a classic car dealership on Kiely and Stevens Creek Boulevard. Richard's part-time business had grown so much that his lot was overflowing. So with no more space, he parked cars in front of his Los Gatos home. At times, he'd have gems like Rolls-Royce convertibles, Ferraris, or a Mercedes-Benz 300 SEL 6.3 sitting there—together, they were worth more than the house.

Brian and Richard were having a drink together at the Grog, a Los Gatos bar and restaurant they went to frequently.

"My neighbors must think I'm a drug dealer," Richard said with a smile.

"It's time to find a bigger lot."

Ken Keegan Auto Imports had decided to move from the corner of Pageant Way and East Main Street in Los Gatos. This was a perfect location for Richard to move his classic car business and solve his space problem. The corner had been the home of car dealerships since 1933, when Cecil Spotswood, mayor of Los Gatos from 1944 to 1946, operated Spotswood Dodge. Ken Keegan took over the space in 1959 with a Volvo dealership that also sold Triumphs, Sunbeams, and BMWs. Richard negotiated a long-term contract with Cecil's daughter Minnie Spotswood, subject to approval by the city of Los Gatos.

Things looked promising.

When Richard met with city officials, his plans came to a screeching halt. It turned out that used car dealerships were no longer allowed in Los Gatos. So, if he wanted to operate a car dealership in town, he'd need a new car dealer license. Without that and a service department that could provide new car warranty service and repairs, he wouldn't be getting a business permit.

Now what?

Two years earlier, Richard and his wife Laurie had been in the market for a new Porsche. They drove to Anderson-Behel Porsche Audi on Stevens Creek Boulevard.

Brian managed that dealership.

Brian had joined the sales staff of Anderson-Behel on his 29th birthday. On his third day, he walked into the office with a signed contract in hand. The two sales managers thought it was a joke. No one had ever sold a car that fast. And, on top of that, it was a car that had been on the lot for a long time: a model 914/6, a mid-engined, two-seat roadster powered by a flat-six engine. No one liked it, and that's why no one had bought it.

Until Brian showed up with a signed contract.

There must be some mistake, the sales managers thought.

When he handed them the customer's check, it sank in—the new salesman really had sold a car. And he'd sold it for the full asking price—no discount.

"How bad do you want to sell this car Brian?" said one sales manager.

"I don't understand, isn't this what I am supposed to do, sell cars?"

"No, we're asking how bad you want to sell it?" said the other sales manager.

"I'm just doing what you hired me to do. I don't understand?"

"Okay Brian, around here, this is how it works. If you want to sell a car, you split the commission with us. That's the way it works."

"Well, that doesn't make sense to me, but do whatever you do. I just want to sell cars."

Brian knew this wasn't right, and it bothered him. He decided to say something to the general manager, Bob Wilson. The next day, he walked upstairs to the general manager's office and stood in the doorway. Mr. Wilson looked up and said, "Come on in, what can I do for you?"

"My name is Brian Burnett. I ran a Pontiac dealership in Oklahoma for a couple years and worked for Bob Sykes Dodge down the street for a while before I started here a few days ago."

"Sure, I know who you are. I've heard a little about you."

"Look, I don't want to rock the boat, but you've got a couple crooks working for you downstairs. Yesterday I sold a 914/6, and they told me if I really wanted to sell the car, I had to give them half my commission. I asked around the lot and found out they are doing this to all the sales staff."

Mr. Wilson looked at Brian for a moment, nodded, and then stood up abruptly. "Wait here in my office a few minutes. I'll be right back."

About 15 minutes later, Mr. Wilson returned.

"Brian, I want to thank you for speaking up about this. You're the first one to say anything. I've suspected something like this for some time but didn't understand why no one complained. So, your new office is downstairs. Here's the keys."

"What do you mean, my new office?"

"You're my new sales manager."

From that day on, Brian managed the dealership as if he owned the place. In just a short time, he took Anderson-Behel from a sales rank of 68th to the number one Porsche Audi dealership in the nation. This wouldn't be the last time he'd make a dealership number one or the last time he'd have to sell unpopular cars.

One day, Brian was on the lot of the Anderson-Behel dealership, checking his inventory. He heard the Ferrari engine before the car ever came into view. He smiled and looked up when the white Ferrari 330 GTS pulled onto the dealership lot and the driver got out.

"My name's Richard Rivoir. I'm a real estate developer here in the area, and I'm interested in a new Porsche."

"Nice to meet you. My name is Brian Burnett, and I'm the sales manager. What's the story on the Ferrari?"

"Quite a car, isn't it? I've got a few collectibles." By now, Laurie had slid out of the passenger side of the car, and Brian said hello.

"Were you thinking of trading in the Ferrari?"

"Sure, I like the Ferrari, but it's not a good everyday driver, and I need something my wife Laurie and I can drive daily. So we're looking for a Porsche."

The boys made a deal, Richard and Laurie had a new gemini blue Porsche Targa, and Brian was happy to have a Ferrari on his lot. All were happy, at least for the time being.

Brian remembered the aftermath of the deal when Mr. Anderson, part owner of the dealership, saw the Ferrari on the showroom floor. "Mr. Anderson walked in one day and said, 'What's that Ferrari doing in the showroom?' I told him it was a trade-in, and that upset him. 'We don't sell Ferraris, we don't know anything about them, and we don't want them in here.'"

A couple of weeks later, the Ferrari sold for an $8,000 profit, more than any Porsche ever made. Mr. Anderson was impressed. "Looks like I was wrong. You made a great deal. Maybe we can do some more of those."

After buying the Porsche, Richard and Laurie moved to Los Gatos and became Brian's neighbors. Separated from his wife and going through a divorce, Brian developed a close friendship with them and enjoyed hanging out together. "We were like the Three Musketeers and became the best of friends." Richard and Brian talked about Ferraris and other classic cars, and Laurie enjoyed socializing with them. They'd hardly ever miss a Friday night dinner at the Grog & Sirloin, a Los Gatos bar and restaurant.

In 1975, the Grog became infamous as the birthplace of the Pet Rock. Brian remembered being there the night it happened. "I was sitting at the bar, having dinner. Gary Dahl, an advertising executive, was listening to friends complain about cleaning up after their pets. He said, 'You need a pet that won't create such problems.' Everyone had their own version of what kind of animal that should be. Gary got their attention when he said, 'What about a rock?' After all, he reasoned, a pet rock would not need to be fed, walked, bathed, or groomed, would never be disobedient, and never get sick or die. We all had the opportunity to invest that evening. We either didn't take him seriously or thought it would never succeed. Gary ended up making a lot of money."

What started as a joke ended up generating sales of more than 1 million Pet Rocks. Each rock cost only a few cents to manufacture and sold for $4 each. The fad ended after six months, but a company owning the rights to the Pet Rock reintroduced it 37 years later. Today, they sell for between $19.95 and $39.99.

At the Grog, Brian and Richard would have a conversation that would shape the future of their lives.

"Brian, I've signed a lease for the Ken Keegan lot. It's a great location, but Los Gatos won't allow a used car dealership in town anymore. To operate at this location, I need a new car dealership that includes warranty service and repairs."

Both Brian and Richard knew Vern Keil, the manager of Modern Classic Motors (MCM), the West Coast Ferrari distributor owned by Bill Harrah. MCM was responsible for appointing new Ferrari dealerships.

"What do you think Brian, shall we talk to Vern and see if we can get a dealership?"

Brian smiled. He was hooked.

Vern had been friends with Richard's dad for years, and Richard remembered visiting MCM with his dad in the past. Recently, he'd become familiar with how MCM operated as a distributor/dealer of Ferraris and occasionally helped them by purchasing a Ferrari and delivering it to a dealer in another state. Through California Imports, he also bought one or two Ferraris a year from MCM.

Brian also knew Vern and had discussed his own interest in a Ferrari dealership with him. He recalled his first telephone conversation with Vern.

"I never beat around the bush. The first time I spoke with Vern, I introduced myself, told him I managed the Porsche/Audi dealership in Northern California and wanted to start a Ferrari dealership in Los Gatos. He said he'd never heard of Los Gatos and asked how old I was. When I answered 33, he told me, 'You don't need a Ferrari dealership. They don't sell many cars, and you can't make money doing this.' Not the response I'd been after, but it didn't discourage me."

Even though both had approached Vern several times and were rejected every time, it didn't stop them from wanting to try again. What did they have to lose? So both continued to call. Vern was always friendly and polite but always insisted a Ferrari dealership wasn't right for either of them.

Vern tended to pick successful car dealers with an existing business selling cars from other manufacturers. He couldn't remember someone as young as Brian or Richard ever asking for a Ferrari dealership.

"I have a lease on a great location and an established banking relationship," Richard told Vern. And when Brian had the opportunity, he reminded Vern he'd turned Anderson-Behel into the number one Porsche Audi dealer in the nation. And they both reminded him they were good at selling used cars and didn't see how the dealership could fail.

Vern's response was usually the same. "You seem like a nice person, so, trust me, you don't need a Ferrari dealership. Older people with a lot of money own these dealerships. Our dealership here, for example, is backed by millions of dollars of something else, understand?"

The *something* else Vern referred to was actually *someone* else: the owner of MCM, Bill Harrah.

In addition to MCM, he owned Harrah's Hotel and Casinos and Harrah's Automobile Collection. He earned a substantial amount from his hotel and casino operations in Nevada and had formed MCM to sell three specific car makes—Ferrari, Rolls-Royce, and Jaguar. While his casinos and hotels made him rich and famous, Harrah enjoyed being a hot-rodder more. He owned many Ferraris and drove them regularly to and from his casinos in Reno and Lake Tahoe.

On a trip to Italy during the 1950s to pick up a Ferrari from the factory, Harrah met Enzo Ferrari. Enzo knew of Harrah's success in gambling casinos, and when he discovered that both had a strong interest in cars, he asked to meet with Harrah. They spent time together, shared car stories, and became friends. Years later, in 1965, Ferrari needed a West Coast distributor, so he naturally reached out to Harrah. As a result, MCM became the distributor responsible for granting Ferrari dealer licenses west of the Mississippi River.

The boys knew what they wanted and whom they had to get it from. And they weren't going to rest until they had it. Their passion and persistence impressed Vern, but he was still reluctant to say yes. Part of the reason he wouldn't was because he liked them. He knew that North American dealers weren't selling many Ferraris. The current dealers made their money selling high volumes of cars manufactured by other companies like BMW, Chevrolet, or Ford, not Ferrari. If they sold an occasional Ferrari, great; if not, it didn't matter to their bottom line.

The dealers enjoyed having a few cool cars on their lot next door, and the owner could drive the Ferrari demo home any time he wanted. In many cases, the prestige of the Ferrari emblem on the building was all they were after. Sales didn't matter. But Vern worried about Richard and Brian, knowing that if they didn't sell cars, the prancing horse emblem couldn't help them pay the rent.

"I'll think about it," Vern would always finish, "and if something changes in the future, we'll talk again."

This time, Richard's mind couldn't stop racing. He had a lease on a great location, but it meant nothing without a new car dealership. He was determined to come up with a solution.

So no matter how often Vern told Richard and Brian what a bad idea a Ferrari dealership was, they had a comeback for every objection. They made phone call after phone call. Worn out and realizing they were not about to quit, he caved in and told the boys to come up to Reno and he'd see what he could do.

Brian and Richard grinned from ear to ear like schoolboys as they cruised in Brian's Porsche up Highway 101 through San Francisco and over the Bay Bridge toward Reno. They arrived earlier than scheduled at Harrah's MCM, ready to make their dream come true. Waiting impatiently in the lobby, they saw Vern walking toward them and almost ran up to greet him. Instead, with smiles stretched until their cheeks hurt, they shook his hand like proper businessmen.

Vern was tall and wore a white shirt and tie. The boys were dressed in blue jeans and polo shirts and wondered if they should have dressed more formally. As they stood in the lobby, they made small talk to break the ice.

"Let's take a walk," Vern finally said and took them on a tour of MCM. This included the shop where Harrah's engineers and mechanics worked on his cars, the showroom floor, and the sales lot.

The workshop could handle a dozen cars and had linoleum tiles that sparkled like a recently scrubbed hospital floor. Harrah was rumored to be a perfectionist, and his mechanics' work area confirmed it.

Brian and Richard found it easy to talk to Vern. The three of them had a passion for Ferraris and classic cars in general.

"As a dealer, Harrah owned many Ferraris, some of which are in his auto museum," said Vern. "He drove them through the desert on his way to and from Lake Tahoe and Reno. Rumor has it that at times he drove so fast, his bodyguards couldn't keep up. And if a bodyguard fell too far behind and lost track of him, he just might be fired. Harrah may be known for his casinos and hotels, but he's always been a hot-rodder."

"Bodyguards?" asked Richard.

"Well fellows, Mr. Harrah is the head of one of the most valuable companies in the world. As a public company listed on the New York Stock Exchange with a value around $300 million, he has to be protected."

The discussion turned to a Northern California Ferrari dealership. Vern had probably made up his mind about the dealership already, but he tested them anyway.

"Did you think about what I told you, that these dealerships don't sell many cars and won't make any money?"

Brian and Richard had listened to Vern, but to them, the notion that you couldn't sell Ferraris in America and were bound to lose money made no sense.

"Vern, we heard what you said, but we still believe Los Gatos is the ideal location for a Ferrari dealership. It's in the heart of Silicon Valley and near Highway 17, the main road to the beach. Other car dealers have been successful from this corner in the past, and the nearest Ferrari dealerships are 50 miles north or 60 miles south. We've got experience selling cars, and we don't see how the dealership can fail."

"Look, I don't want to see you boys get in trouble. Like I said before, the other dealers don't rely solely on Ferrari sales to pay their bills. They have other lines that are the moneymakers."

"Vern, we appreciate that. So here's what we're willing to do. If you're right and we can't sell Ferraris and become your number one dealer in 90 days, we'll give everything back."

"What?"

"I said, if we are not your number one dealer in 90 days, we'll tear up the contract and give you back whatever's left. No harm, no foul, and no questions asked. What do you say?"

Vern was at a crossroads and found it hard to argue. He had nothing to lose. He had ample good reason to want to move the Ferraris sitting in his warehouse but didn't want to see Brian and Richard get hurt. He was trying to figure out how to deny them once more but was wavering. Maybe letting them fail was the answer. Then they'd learn their lesson and see you couldn't make money with a Ferrari dealership.

"Well, those terms do give you guys a way out, which is what I always wanted in the first place. Okay, let's review the contract, sign it, and pick out your car."

They tried controlling their excitement, but it was almost impossible.

"Thank you, Vern."

It took a while to go through the dealership contract. When they finished, Brian and Richard realized that while they may be running the business, Ferrari controlled everything. They had the right to use the Ferrari name, logo, reputation, goodwill, and so on but had no ownership rights in any of these things. The use of these items could be revoked at any time if they did not follow the rules established by Ferrari. For example, the business could not be sold to anyone unless Ferrari approved of the new owner. There was a lot of fine print, but getting the dealership was the goal, and whatever had to be signed to accomplish that seemed okay. Some 20 years later, the fine print would come back to haunt Brian, but at the time, 20 years seemed like an eternity.

Finally, after listening to the explanations, the contract was signed.

"Okay, the contract requires you to purchase at least one car to get started. Let's go out to the warehouse and see which one you'd like."

As they turned and started to leave for the warehouse, Vern said, "Oh, there is one problem."

They stopped and looked back.

"Someone made a mistake ordering the cars we have right now. The only model we have in stock are 308 GT4s, and they are unusual colors; none are red."

No red Ferraris?

How could this be? How many Ferraris had appeared in a movie or television series that weren't red? Ferrari Formula One race cars came in one color—Ferrari red (Rossa Corsa). More importantly, customers identified Ferrari with red—it was the color everyone wanted.

And only GT4s?

That model featured goofy-looking angular lines instead of the smooth curves Ferrari lovers expected. Bertone had designed the body-work instead of Pininfarina, the designer on earlier models, and not many people liked the change. No wonder Vern was stuck with them.

Richard shrugged his shoulders and lifted his eyebrows, and Brian couldn't have cared less. They were Ferraris, and that's all that mattered. They looked at each other as if to say, nothing's going to stop us now.

They followed Vern on the five-minute drive to the warehouse, parked in front, and walked toward the entrance. Vern stopped at the door and apologized once more about the models and colors.

Then he opened the door but was greeted with nothing but darkness. The warehouse lights weren't working.

Vern had to go back to his car for a flashlight.

"Here, this will help you see a little better," Vern said as he handed them a flashlight. "I need to get back to the office and attend to some other business. Come back to my office when you've finished and let me know which car you want. Make sure you lock the door on your way out."

It was obvious no one had looked at the Ferraris for a long time; they were covered with dust in utter darkness at the back of the ware-house. Stumbling around with a flashlight in the dark should have been upsetting. But they were excited; they enjoyed being around the cars. The Ferraris were shoved up against each other and looked abandoned. They had front and rear plastic shipping bumpers, but most were scratched and dented so badly that they'd have to be repainted before they could be sold.

"Doesn't it look like the workers purposely banged these cars into each other?" Richard wondered. "There are a lot of dings and scratches on them. Somewhere along the line, someone was very careless."

But even with the cars in need of minor repairs and new paint, they couldn't stop thinking about the dealership. They maneuvered around in the dark as best they could and eventually settled on a light green car with tan interior and a black boxer bottom. It was the best-looking Ferrari in the warehouse. The rest were terrible color combinations, even in the dark.

As they locked up the warehouse and walked back to their car, Brian stopped suddenly.

"Richard let's talk about this for a minute. Why don't you call the bank and see if they'll loan us enough to buy 'em all?"

"Are you crazy?" Richard exclaimed.

"It may be the only way we can become the number one dealer in 90 days."

"That's a big commitment Brian. And some of those cars don't look that great. It's nuts to take 19 cars we may not be able to sell."

"I know it'll work. The banker you introduced me to was excited about financing Ferraris, and he'll own them until they're sold."

Richard agreed to try.

Brian and Richard returned to MCM and asked Vern's assistant if there was a phone they could use to make a private call. She escorted them down the hall to an empty office where Brian closed the door and Richard made his call. After explaining the opportunity, the banker was on board. The boys walked down the hall to Vern's office with a confident strut and heads held high.

Brian grew up respecting his Uncle George, who always told him, "If you're gonna be a bear, be a grizzly." He remembered that as he turned the corner and walked into Vern's office.

Vern looked up.

"Well, boys, which one do you want?"

Brian looked him straight in the eyes.

"We'll take 'em all."

Vern leaned back in his chair as far as it would go, raised his hands high, and locked them together behind his head.

"All? Why on earth would you do that? These are unpopular colors of an unwanted model. You'll have a hard time selling any of them."

But they wanted a dealership badly. Without it, the city of Los Gatos would not let them open shop, and Richard would be stuck with a lease for property he could not use. City officials had made it clear—no used car lots: only a new car dealership with a factory-authorized service and repair department would do.

"We understand your concerns Vern, but we can make this work. We're willing to commit to taking all the GT4s you can't sell. If you give us a chance, we'll fix your inventory issues."

While this certainly got Vern's attention, he hesitated.

"You just don't get it. It will be near impossible to sell these unwanted cars. If you're not careful, you'll be out of business in no time."

Brian swallowed hard before repeating with even more confidence, "We'll take 'em all."

They had a signed contract, so Vern had no choice but to approve. However, he did stipulate that they could take only four cars now and that the rest would be delivered only if these were sold. They agreed, shook hands, and left Vern's office to head home.

Meanwhile, Vern sat at his desk, head in hands, thinking about what he'd done and promising himself he'd never do it again. From now on, if he needed another dealership, he'd go back to appointing a car dealer already successful selling another brand of car. No more young start-ups. Ever.

Persistence paid off for Brian and Richard. They had become Northern California's newest Ferrari dealer.

"Once there was a signed Ferrari dealer contract, Richard and I agreed on a simple plan. We'd run the business together, he'd focus on buying cars, I'd focus on selling them, and we'd split everything 50/50."

How could anything go wrong? Richard had the banking contacts, while Brian could manage a sales team and build the dealership. And, most importantly, they both believed they could accomplish anything together.

The following day, Brian told his boss, Bob Wilson, that he was leaving. Mr. Wilson called part owner Wes Behel to let him know. Mr. Behel didn't usually socialize with the staff, but he asked Brian to lunch.

"I've never taken anybody to lunch who was thinking of leaving the dealership. It's almost killing me to tell you this, but you've done an amazing job here, and I don't want you to leave. If you stay, I'll make sure you become part of this place. I know you'll do well because you know how to make the place run right. And you know how to make money. None of my managers have been able to do that in the past."

Brian recalled feeling like an idiot passing up the chance to become a bigger part of Anderson-Behel, but his passion was elsewhere.

"I'm sorry, Mr. Behel, but I gotta do this."

On the way home that night, Brian couldn't help but second-guess his decision. After all, he was living a pretty darn good life. He was walking away from a secure job that generated a steady high income. He thought he'd be able to make a decent living working with Richard, but it was a risk compared to Anderson-Behel. Then he recalled the childhood memory of Jim Kimberly firing up that Ferrari V-12 engine. And his decision was final.

Brian and Richard met to start planning what they were going to do. First, they needed a business name. Richard had recently seen a TV commercial for a woman's perfume called Lancôme of Paris. He was intrigued that someone would put their location after their product name. So why not Ferrari of Los Gatos? At the time, besides Lancôme, he couldn't think of anyone else doing it—especially not car dealerships. Ferrari thought differently, advising him the store name should use the same format as other dealers'—city before make, that is, Los Gatos Ferrari.

Destined to be different, Brian and Richard disagreed. Their dealership became Ferrari of Los Gatos. Persistence paid off again, and it didn't take long for other Ferrari dealerships to do the same—but Ferrari of Los

Gatos was the first. Today, North American Ferrari dealerships follow the naming sequence Brian and Richard coined in 1976.

And Ferrari of Los Gatos would be different in many more ways than just its name.

CHAPTER FOUR

Gentlemen, Start Your Engines

(1976)

FOR WEEKS, THE LOCAL NEWSPAPER HAD ADVERTISED A NEW FERRARI dealership was coming to town. It was the summer of 1976 when Ferrari of Los Gatos opened its doors in this small town on Silicon Valley's outskirts. A steady stream of excited onlookers surrounded the cars for sale. Wide-eyed and speechless, they stood overwhelmed at so many Ferraris together in the same place. Modern Classic Motors (MCM) had removed the scratches and dings and touched up the paint, so even the strange colors looked good.

Visitors were so impressed that they couldn't wait to tell their friends what they had seen, bringing even more visitors. On weekends, wall-to-wall crowds made it difficult to move around the lot or the showroom

The corner of Pageant Way and East Main Street, Los Gatos, California.
Personal photo Brian Burnett

floor. Ferrari of Los Gatos was an overnight success at drawing large crowds.

The trouble was, while the visitors shared a passion and interest in the cars, most of them had come to check out the cool cars—not buy. It was great to have such large crowds, but Brian and Richard had committed to buy MCM's slow-moving inventory of unpopular models and had to make good on that promise.

Vern's warning about how difficult it would be to sell unpopular models in unpopular colors echoed in Richard's mind. Vern may have been right that it wouldn't be easy, but Richard and Brian had a can-do attitude and didn't become discouraged. And although, as they expected, almost everyone said, "I really wanted a red one," the dealership developed comebacks to overcome objections. For this one, it was, "Now, why would you want the same color as everyone else?"

Stunned and unsure of how to react, potential customers had to think about whether they wanted to be like everyone else. Customers with outgoing personalities realized that they didn't mind being different. After all, just owning a Ferrari made you stand out. The domino effect kicked in, and others reasoned that if someone else bought a Ferrari that wasn't red, they could too. Excitement about the unusual colors grew, and cars started selling.

And yet the cars weren't exactly flying off the lot. At the time, people were still reeling from the 1973 recession that had lasted through 1975. This recession had turned into stagflation, or when high unemployment and high inflation take place together. The stock market crash was still fresh in people's minds, and it would be years before most investments recovered. Everyone was struggling financially, even the income brackets of Los Gatos.

In the wake of the 1973 oil crisis, the Dow Jones Industrial Average lost 45 percent of its value during the 1973–1974 stock market crash. President Nixon asked gas stations to close on Saturday nights and all day Sunday. When they were open, long lines at the pump were common in many states. The American Automobile Association reported that 20 percent of American gasoline stations had no fuel in the last week of February 1974. In California, motorists bought gas based on the last digit of their license plates. Those with an odd number or a vanity plate could purchase gas only on odd-numbered days, while those with an even number could buy only on even-numbered days.

The government imposed a national speed limit of 55 mph, and by 1980, heavy domestic luxury cars were no longer manufactured. Instead, automakers started offering more efficient four-cylinder engines and diesel-powered passenger cars. Even auto racing groups began conserving. In 1974, NASCAR reduced all race distances by 10 percent and canceled the 24 Hours of Daytona and 12 Hours of Sebring races.

Not exactly the right environment for selling an expensive, fast luxury car.

And in 1976, not too many individuals could afford a sports car for weekend drives, weather permitting. The average annual income was $12,686, and a new home cost about $48,000. Times were tough, and people were hesitant to take chances, especially with a car that cost more than a house. Steve Jobs, Steve Wozniak, and Ronald Wayne founded a start-up called Apple Computer. Nervous about the economy, Wayne believed the company would never take off and sold his stake in Apple for $2,300 after 12 days. That speaks volumes about people's confidence in the economy back then.

Richard and Brian weren't intimidated by these odds, but they knew they needed to try something different. The biting question was *what?*

In the car business, demonstration drives allow sales staff to point out the car's features and apply traditional sales tactics to a captive audience for a few minutes. Ferrari of Los Gatos staff gave demonstration rides all day long. There were plenty of customers asking for a demo drive—a good thing, right?

Not necessarily.

Life lessons can come from unexpected sources. Sometimes people or coincidences come into our lives to teach and guide us.

One day, a young lawyer walked into the showroom.

"I'd like to test drive a Ferrari."

Naturally, the salesman replied, "Sure, let me get the keys to our demo car." The lawyer drove the car around town with a big smile, and the salesman tried to convince him to buy. Ten minutes later, the lawyer parked the car back on the lot, tossed the keys to the salesman, and said, "Thank you."

Following him to the sidewalk, the salesman asked, "Can I answer any questions or work up a quote for you?"

The reply shocked him.

"Oh, I didn't want to buy a Ferrari, just wanted to drive one."

When Brian heard what happened, he knew right away what needed to change. Effective immediately, any customer who wanted to take a car on a test drive would have to settle for the passenger seat. From here on out, only sales staff would drive the cars.

Brian also knew that this alone would not make people buy cars. He had to figure out a way to turn lookers into buyers.

Most owners of Ferrari dealerships were successful in selling other car makes and models. Their Ferrari lots were the icing on the cake. Like Vern at MCM had warned, "Dealers don't make money selling Ferraris; they're backed by something else." The other owners didn't need to sell Ferraris to make a living and didn't want their customers drifting off the BMW, Chevy, or Ford lots. That's where they made their profits. Requiring cash deals helped keep their customers where they wanted them. If you couldn't pay cash or weren't rich, famous, or at least dressing the part, you likely felt out of place on their Ferrari lots. The other dealers seemed to be saying, "Come look at my Ferraris if you are part of our exclusive club. Otherwise, stay on my lot full of average cars for ordinary people."

Not so at Ferrari of Los Gatos.

Richard and Brian decided the only new cars they'd sell would be Ferraris. To make this lucrative, they needed to convince the average person that a Ferrari was affordable. First things first: they changed their image. The sales staff dressed casually in polo shirts and jeans to make customers feel comfortable, welcomed, and at ease while discussing the car of their dreams. Brian believed that the perfect time to do business with customers was when they were relaxed. It was a good move, but it didn't solve the biggest obstacle.

How does the average person pay for a Ferrari?

The average individual in 1976 did not have cash saved for a down payment on an expensive car. Searching for a solution, Brian glanced down the street at the Los Gatos library parking lot and recalled his high school days selling cars to students and friends. And now, here he was, across the street some 15 years later, selling the car of his dreams.

Back in the day, Brian would drive around Santa Cruz on weekends looking for classic cars in someone's driveway or garage. When he found one, he'd walk up to the house and ring the doorbell. If the owner was willing to sell (and many times they were), Brian found a buyer back in Los Gatos. He remembered that many of his teenage customers couldn't pay cash either. But if they had a small amount of money along with a car to trade in, a deal was done.

Next, Brian would find a buyer for the trade-in. While he made only a small profit on each car, he doubled the number of transactions and increased his income by taking a trade-in.

Could this be the solution he needed?

Next differentiator? The sales staff in jeans and polo shirts would accept trade-ins as a down payment. Customers liked the idea; they didn't have to come up with all cash. The sales staff figured out quickly that they could make a second commission when they sold the trade-in. And the trade-ins kept the lot full of other classic cars for sale.

Most other Ferrari dealers were doing the opposite—cash only and no trade-ins. Even in California, the average person thought you had to be independently wealthy to drive one of Enzo's cars. If you weren't, you could go by, look, dream a little, but never buy one. Brian wanted to change that perception. At Ferrari of Los Gatos, anyone should be able to own a Ferrari.

"We need to offer a financing program," Brian told Richard. "Payments for a Ferrari should be no different than a Ford Mustang." It wasn't rocket science, just numbers, and it wasn't the first time someone in the car business realized it.

Twenty years earlier, a Ford sales manager named Lee Iacocca had faced a similar challenge. Sales of new Fords in 1956 were lousy everywhere, and in his Pennsylvania territory, they were horrible. So he came up with a plan: any customer could buy a 1956 Ford for a 20 percent down payment, followed by three years of $56 monthly payments. He called it "56 for 56." At the time, financing cars for more than a year was a new concept, and his idea was a great success.

Within three months, his Philadelphia territory went from last in sales to first. The plan was so successful that Robert McNamara, the Ford vice president who would later become the U.S. secretary of defense under President John F. Kennedy, adopted it as a national program. He reported the plan sold 75,000 extra cars that year. Iacocca became district manager of Washington, D.C., and suddenly his future became a whole lot brighter.

Years later, Iacocca became CEO of the Chrysler Corporation, saved it from financial ruin, and masterminded the minivan's creation while overseeing the renovation of Ellis Island. He became an automotive legend, and many Americans once wished he would run for president of the United States.

Like Iacocca, Richard and Brian wanted to be number one. They had an agreement with Bill Harrah to take the unpopular 308 GT4 model Ferraris in his warehouse, and they had to make good on that commitment. To do so, they would have to overcome the fact that other dealers had convinced everyone that Ferraris were only for the rich and famous.

Knowing it would be difficult to overcome this perception, the dealership needed a program to shatter the myth and show the average person they could afford the most prestigious car in the world. They'd solved the down-payment issue with trade-ins; now they needed a long-term financing program.

Like it or not, finance is the heart of any business. Does the company have enough capital to cover expenses, pay its employees, and invest in enough inventory, equipment, and facilities? If not, most start-ups don't succeed. Ferrari of Los Gatos was bootstrapped with only $20,000 of working capital, half of it borrowed from friends and relatives and no deep pockets for more.

Fortunately, Richard had established a good banking relationship from the beginning. The initial inventory-flooring loan from Bank of America allowed them to buy cars with borrowed funds, make interest-only payments, and pay back the loan after selling the vehicle. Even though this helped fund the initial inventory, it did not address customer financing.

Other dealers did not offer financing, so customers had to arrange a bank loan independently or pay cash. And, at the time, when bankers heard the word "Ferrari," they wanted to run out the back door. Brian remembered how bankers knew nothing about the cars, and that made them skeptical. "Ferraris were like a black cat to a banker, they didn't understand them, and that made them afraid to get near financing them. But we talked our bank into financing them, and boy, did they make a lot of money."

Luck came the boys' way when a friend of Richard's mentioned a new bank to him. "You've got to come over to Santa Cruz and meet my friend Bill Winterhalder. He heads the County Bank of Santa Cruz auto finance department and manages all the car dealership business. He's loaning $50,000 to truckers driving diesel freeway haulers, and these guys don't even own a home."

Brian and Richard raced over the hill as soon as they could to meet with Bill. He liked what they presented, and County Bank of Santa Cruz offered to replace the flooring provided by Bank of America and add a unique program for Ferrari of Los Gatos customers. It turned out Bill was a car guy at heart. He loved to visit the dealership and hang out with Brian and Richard. No matter what they wanted or needed, his reply was, "Yeah, no problem." While traditional banks would not finance used cars, for Bill at County Bank of Santa Cruz, the excitement of classic Ferraris and other exotic vehicles seemed to make it okay.

While other car dealers owned their used cars and financed only their new vehicles, Ferrari of Los Gatos went a different direction—they borrowed against everything.

Richard recalled how much Bill helped them. "Looking back, there were two things that made us all that money. First, there was great inflation going on, and that made the value of the cars we bought go up. Second, we found a bank that would finance collectible cars."

County Bank of Santa Cruz understood the business model of Ferrari of Los Gatos and, unlike most other banks, seemed eager to loan money secured by the most popular car in the world. Banks love to lend money when security is high, and a Ferrari's value kept going up.

The bankers were secure and felt there was no long-term risk.

One could argue that Ferrari of Los Gatos took advantage of the banker's positive state of mind. But isn't that what start-ups are supposed to do—leverage available resources?

County Bank of Santa Cruz put together a program that mirrored a lease. While car leasing was not typical, Bill was familiar with a company that leased a few cars in the early 1970s. While it was technically a loan secured by the vehicle, a customer could buy a car with a relatively small down payment or trade-in and 35 monthly payments that anyone with average credit could afford. The loan contained a final balloon payment in the thirty-sixth month. If the borrower could not afford to make the balloon payment, the bankers would refinance or write a new loan. Since Ferraris were going up in value as time went by, the numbers worked. It was no different than what home owners do all the time—refinance.

Ferrari of Los Gatos named their new financing program the "35-and-one plan." Like Iacocca's "56 for 56," the 35-and-one plan stimulated sales. With this new financing plan, dreamers became owners. And wealthy individuals who didn't want to tie up their money in a Ferrari or other classic car could use the program as well.

The words on the ad that ran in newspapers and magazines across the country read, "The Possible Dream." And at Ferrari of Los Gatos, a customer could walk in, purchase a Ferrari, and drive it home—something unheard of at most other dealers across the country.

Now the boys had to keep their lot stocked with cars. To do so, Richard would meet wholesalers or dealers at the Los Angeles International Airport, purchase their vehicles, and load them on a car hauler to make the 345-mile drive to Ferrari of Los Gatos. The demand got so high that these trips were taking place twice a week. It didn't take long for Richard and Brian to become the number one dealer on the West Coast. And it took only 40 days to sell every single one of those unpopular cars that no other dealer would buy from MCM.

The possible dream.

Some people call them dream cars: Ferrari, Rolls Royce, Maserati, Lamborghini, Bentley, Mercedes, Porsche. But if owning one of these cars is not just a dream, but your goal, come see us.

We have the finest selection of automotive exotica for sale in the Western United States. Including a wide selection of new Ferraris. Chances are, we have what you want now, or will have it soon.

And we've got a variety of purchase and lease plans to make driving that special car a lot easier than you'd dream possible.

Give us a call. There's no need to go on dreaming.

Ferrari
of Los Gatos

Factory authorized Ferrari sales and service
66 East Main Street Los Gatos, CA 95030
(408) 354-4000

This advertisement ran in newspapers and magazines throughout the country. *Ferrari of Los Gatos when owned by Brian Burnett*

How'd they done that? Vern wondered but never asked. He just enjoyed the fact that he could restock his inventory with the right models and colors.

And Vern wasn't ready for what came next. Unfortunately, neither was the Ferrari factory in Maranello.

CHAPTER FIVE

Building a Business

(1976–1977)

SELLING THE UNWANTED CARS IN BILL HARRAH'S WAREHOUSE AT Modern Classic Motors (MCM) made Ferrari of Los Gatos number one quickly. Now, the boys had a new challenge.

They'd run out of new Ferraris to sell.

Their success created the highest demand MCM had experienced. Vern sent the largest order he'd ever placed to Maranello, and the Ferrari factory responded with a lead time spanning months.

Now what?

They got up early one morning and put their heads together. They needed new Ferraris, the factory could not deliver them for months, so where else could they get the cars they needed?

The only place where new Ferraris existed was on the lots of the other North American dealers. So the plan was to call the larger New York and Texas dealers first, then make their way across the country. Next, they'd hit Chicago, Detroit, St. Louis, Atlanta, and even Hawaii. Brian remembered how the dealers responded to his calls.

"This is Brian Burnett from Ferrari of Los Gatos in California. Do you have any cars we can buy?"

The typical response?

"Why, what's going on in California?"

"We need cars to sell while waiting for the factory to restock us."

Ferrari of Los Gatos was calling everyone. Not the right color? Not a popular model? Doesn't matter. Send it west.

In those early days, Brian and Richard were incurable optimists. Failure was not an option, and together they believed they could accomplish anything. They tried new things, continued to differentiate, and focused on whatever it took to be successful.

The front corner of the dealership had a glass-walled showroom. Richard maintained a real estate office on the right-hand side, and Brian ran car sales from an office on the street side. The two offices created bookends to the showroom. It didn't take long, and they were selling cars at a feverish pace.

Times were good, and it seemed like no matter what obstacle presented itself, these two young men could overcome it. They were making a ton of money—Brian estimated it was enough to buy a Los Gatos house every 90 days.

They established a service department by hiring their school friend Mark to be service manager and added a mechanic. Shortly after that, they had to hire two more mechanics because the business increased so much. All four of the service staff graduated from a factory training center and became Ferrari certified. The company was on fire, generating profits from both sales and service.

They discovered free advertising by driving cars up and down the street. The roar of a Ferrari engine made people on the street stop and look, and it brought the employees and customers out of the neighboring stores and offices. Of course, everyone wanted to see what was going on, and before long, people were flocking into the dealership. Just like the car enthusiasts who followed Ferraris to racetracks around the world, San Francisco Bay Area residents wanted to be part of whatever was happening on the corner of Pageant Way and East Main Street.

In Sunday papers across the country, advertisements would list three or four new Ferraris and six or eight used Ferraris. The bottom of the ad read, "We Offer More, Ferrari Los Gatos, 66 East Main, 408-354-4000." On Monday, the phone would ring nonstop with calls from all over the United States. Some sales took place over the phone, sight unseen. In those days, there was no way to get pictures to an interested buyer quickly. The personal computer didn't show up until the mid-1980s, fax machines wouldn't be on the scene for another 10 years, and

FERRARI
308 GT/4'S
$299 PER MONTH
for 35 months
2 left, red (SER 0256)
White (SER 0060)
1 balloon of $13,625.15. $3,000
cash or trade + tax & license. Total
cash price $24,090.16
FERRARI OF LOS GATOS
66 E. Main   408/354-4000

Los Angeles Times, **August 5, 1977.** *Ferrari of Los Gatos when owned by Brian Burnett*

the internet didn't go live until 1991. Pencil and paper accompanied by a manila folder were the tools of the trade in the 1970s. Two women in the office had electric typewriters but used them only to produce sale contracts. With only a push-button phone, Brian bought Ferraris worldwide, selling many the same way. Most of the time, he had a buyer before he had the car.

Richard frequently traveled to view and purchase used Ferraris for sale. When he bought one, it was Brian's job to make sure it got sold. If a vehicle checked out, he'd pay for it and drive it back to Los Gatos or arrange to have it shipped. Richard remembered flying to Denver to pick up two Ferrari Dinos. He took a buddy along and a set of walkie-talkie radios—cell phones didn't exist yet. Driving through Utah, they encountered empty roads that seemed to go straight forever. No people, no buildings, and no cars. It wasn't unusual to be cruising through a valley at

140 mph and get passed by the other Dino doing 144 mph. "Those were great times. We had a lot of fun."

Richard met two young kids, both named Steve, who founded a Silicon Valley business in 1976 as well. Their start-up was a computer company, and most people didn't understand what they were trying to do. They couldn't afford an expensive car at the time, but they sure enjoyed checking them out. They ended up taking their company public four years later at a valuation of $1 billion. When he read about it in the newspaper, Richard thought for sure they'd be back to buy a pair of the most expensive Ferraris on the lot. "The first time I saw them after the IPO [initial public offering], I was ready to order them two of the latest and greatest Ferraris. But, instead, they just wanted to hang out with me and look at the cars we had on the lot. Nothing had changed." Richard remembered that when an employee walked by with a Ferrari of Los Gatos T-shirt on, one of them said, "That's what we want. We'll trade you a couple of our tank top shirts for a couple of your tee shirts." Richard and his wife Laurie ended up with tank tops showing a rainbow apple on the back with a bite taken out.

Steve Jobs and Steve Wozniak would go on to change the world and how human beings communicate. And their company, Apple Computer, became the most valuable business in the world—that is, until recently, when Amazon became number one.

It was an incredible historical time, and Ferrari of Los Gatos was in the middle of it.

"When Brian and I got on the phone and put something in our heads, we'd make it happen. We had a great relationship, and nothing was going to stop us, nothing."

The crazy money kept coming in, a lot of it in cash. Brian and Richard were buying classic cars, restoring them, and accumulating them in a building they shared downtown. While Richard preferred old-model Mercedes and foreign car models, Brian liked big Packard and Buick model cars. He was the hot-rodder of the two, and putting hot rods together was Brian's passion.

Brian built a large home on a two-acre Los Gatos lot. It included a tennis court, a swimming pool, and a creek running through the back.

The front circular driveway could fit about a dozen cars, and there were usually classic Ferraris among them. There were times the vehicles were worth as much as or more than the house. Brian was living in the fast lane.

Richard lived in a large home in Los Gatos as well and, as a real estate agent, was keenly aware of how lucrative helping buyers and sellers handle real estate transactions could be. The population in Northern California was growing feverishly, causing home values to increase.

Maybe Ferrari of Los Gatos was growing too fast. Managing many transactions at a quick pace wasn't easy. Some cars were purchased and sold before Richard knew anything about them. He told Brian he didn't like that and wanted to be involved in the decision making. After all, their agreement was he would focus on buying cars and Brian would sell them.

Brian didn't like anyone looking over his shoulder and certainly wouldn't let anyone tell him what to do. He was going to run the dealership his way and eventually stopped discussing the business with Richard. The staff noticed the tension. When Brian or Richard saw the other approaching, they'd walk the other way. Eventually, the two weren't even speaking to each other.

When Richard traveled to look at cars, his wife Laurie and Brian continued going to the Grog after work for drinks and dinner. The three of them had gone to the restaurant together for years, so it didn't seem strange to Brian. "It didn't feel out of the ordinary to go to dinner with Laurie, but I think Richard felt this was too cozy a relationship. His jealousy undermined the friendship we once compared to the Three Musketeers and created stress on the business relationship."

There's usually a straw that breaks the camel's back, and Richard's straw dropped on his back while he was in Hawaii.

"I was in the islands for a short vacation with my wife Laurie and had arranged to look at a couple of Ferrari Dinos. After purchasing the two cars, we checked in to the famous Kahala Hilton, a hideaway resort frequented by royalty, heads of state, and Hollywood stars."

It's customary in high-end resorts that luxury cars aren't taken to the parking garage but rather are kept near the front entrance. So that's where the Ferraris ended up. Not only could the valet staff keep an eye on them, but they also made great conversation pieces for guests as they entered or left the resort.

One evening, as Richard and Laurie walked out of the resort lobby, they noticed someone admiring the Ferraris. When they approached, they recognized a familiar face checking out the cars: Tom Selleck, star of *Magnum P.I.*, the popular TV series that featured him driving a red Ferrari 308 around the island of Oahu. The Ferrari 308 became so popular while the show aired that it became known to many as the "Magnum Ferrari," a name it still goes by to this day.

"I sure enjoy watching *Magnum P.I.*," Richard said as they walked up.

"Oh, hi, are these your cars?" Selleck replied.

"Yes, we purchased them yesterday, and we're going to ship them back to our Ferrari dealership in California."

"They're beauties. Not the same model I drive on the show, but I'm sure they're just as much fun."

Richard introduced himself and Laurie to Tom and thanked him for all the free promotion his show was giving Ferrari of Los Gatos. "Your driving a red Ferrari around the Hawaiian Islands is helping us sell them." They laughed and shook hands, and Tom said he hoped they had a great time in Hawaii.

Later, as Richard and Laurie sat having dinner overlooking the ocean, they talked about what a coincidence it was running into Tom Selleck, a person most Americans associated with Ferrari as much as Enzo Ferrari himself, maybe more. Of course, nothing in life is a coincidence, if you know what I mean.

The next day, Richard called Brian.

"I was able to get the Ferraris we wanted. I'll make the arrangements to have them shipped to the mainland. They'll be in the port of Los Angeles in seven to 10 days."

"Richard, we've got buyers for these cars right now. They might not be around in 10 days. So, you better figure out a way to get them here quicker."

"Okay, Brian, I'll see what I can do."

Richard and Laurie had a flight home the next day. They called the airline and discovered there was room for one more pallet in the cargo hold of the 747 jet plane. Richard offered to pay air cargo rates if the two cars could fly on their commercial flight. The airline agreed but only if they could get both cars on one pallet.

They each drove a Ferrari to the airport. When they attempted to put the two cars on one pallet, it was apparent they were not going to fit. "I wanted to show up in Los Gatos with the cars, so I hired an airport mechanic to remove the bumpers. With the front and rear bumpers sitting in the seat, we were able to get the Ferraris on one pallet so they could fly home with us the next day."

Brian was happy to see the cars but not surprised. After all, he and Richard operated with the same mind-set—when something needed to get done, nothing was going to stop them.

"Richard, we've not only got these two cars sold already, but we also sold several other cars while you were gone. We even sold the old Mercedes 300SL that came in on trade."

Richard was visibly shocked. "You knew I wanted to keep that car. It only had 10,000 miles on it. How could you sell it without talking to me first?"

"Well, Richard, we try to move 'em off the lot as fast as we can."

Richard tried to look the other way and let it go, but it kept bothering him. He had to find out the details behind the sale. Reviewing the transaction in the file just upset him more. The selling price of the Mercedes was below market value.

It turns out that Richard never really had the same appetite for risk that Brian did. As Brian took more chances, Richard worried more. Those feelings turned into a lack of trust, and the relationship began to sour. Eventually, Richard felt he had lost the partner he could rely on, and Brian became a liability. Soon, Richard became so uncomfortable that he decided he could no longer work with Brian.

Brian recalled meeting for lunch at Johnny's restaurant at the Courtside Tennis Club to discuss the situation. "I told Richard there was nothing out of the ordinary going on when he traveled and that I was operating the business like I always had. Richard disagreed and said that one of us had to buy the other out. Things in my personal life weren't going that well for me at the time, so we decided that Richard would buy me out."

This wasn't part of Brian's plan when he left a sure thing at Anderson-Behel Porsche Audi. He'd worked hard to build Ferrari of Los Gatos and wished the situation could have been different. Reluctantly, after just four years, Brian left the dealership, and Richard ended up running the business solo.

However, that didn't last for long.

Richard, a real estate man at heart, had never quite left real estate entirely and wanted to devote more time to that business rather than cars. With Brian gone, Richard hoped to run the car dealership from a distance by getting a suitable general manager to run the day-to-day operations. That proved more difficult than he expected, and he soon learned that not all businesses can be successful with an absentee owner.

The dealership sucked him back into a full-time daily routine with even more to do now that Brian was gone. Richard didn't enjoy Ferrari of Los Gatos anymore.

Shortly after he dissolved his partnership with Brian, Richard had enough and sold the business to Norm Nason, a local real estate developer. Norm had always been fascinated by the dealership and how profitable it was. However, Norm needed special knowledge to run the dealership and didn't have it. As a result, the business consumed most of Norm's waking hours seven days a week—he'd stepped into Richard's shoes and was suffering the same fate.

Norm asked Richard to come back, but Richard declined—real estate development was his thing. Norm wasn't pleased about that but couldn't convince Richard otherwise, no matter what he said or did.

Norm realized it was too much for him. Or maybe it was his wife who decided it was too much for him. Brian remembered what Norm had told him. "He said to me, 'At the breakfast table this morning, my wife reminded me that I told her the Ferrari dealership was an investment. She said it has consumed me and that I'm not available to my family anymore. She finished with you need to do something about this, and you need to do it now.'"

Things had not improved, so Norm decided to call a friend.

CHAPTER SIX

I'm Back

(1981)

"BRIAN, THIS IS NORM. I NEED TO TALK WITH YOU."

Brian had been upset that Richard had forced him out of Ferrari of Los Gatos and then sold the business within a few months to someone else. Another real estate agent, no less, rather than a car guy. Richard had known that Brian's heart and soul were still with Ferrari of Los Gatos. Why hadn't he offered it back to him if he didn't want it? Even so, that was Richard's doing, and there was no need to take it out on the new owner. So, he was willing to listen.

"Okay, what's up?"

"Let's meet for lunch. I'll pick you up at 11:30."

Norm pulled up to the curb outside Brian's house. Once in the car, Brian asked, "How are things going?"

"Not well, I'll tell you that."

"Trouble with Ferrari?"

"No, no, nothing like that."

They drove to the Grog. As the hostess walked them to their regular table, she asked Brian, "Where's Laurie and Richard?" Brian just shook his head. They ordered lunch, there was no need for a menu, and Norm got right to the point.

"Brian, I made a mistake buying the Ferrari dealership. It's too much for me. I don't have the kind of car experience needed to run the business."

"So why don't you give it back to Richard?"

"I wouldn't sell it back to Richard if he was the last person on earth. He refused to come back and help me, and that I cannot forgive. So, I want to sell the business to you."

"Well, Norm, I'd love to get the dealership back, but I don't have any money."

Brian remembered Norm's unusual response. "He told me, 'You don't understand. When I left for work this morning, my wife told me that if I don't sell that business today, by God, she'll divorce me tonight.'"

Brian looked at Norm, tilted his head, and shrugged his shoulders. "Norm, I'm flat broke."

"Do you still have property in town?"

"Sure, Norm, I have my house and two rental homes, but they all have big mortgages."

"I don't care about that. Let's finish lunch and go look at your rental houses."

They finished eating and walked out to the parking lot. Brian realized he'd just received an offer for Ferrari of Los Gatos in the same restaurant Richard had made his offer four years earlier. What are the odds? And was it a good omen?

Brian recalled what Norm had told him when they arrived at his three-bedroom rental house. "We parked across the street and sat in the car. Norm was thinking. Staring out the window at the house, without looking at me, he said, 'I have to be able to go home tonight and tell my wife Ferrari of Los Gatos belongs to someone else. If you'll sign the title on this house over to me, the dealership is yours.'

"The offer surprised me. Norm didn't even ask how much the mortgage was.

"I told him, Norm, like I said before, I want the dealership but I don't have any cash. And I'm not even sure what the balance is on the mortgage that will come with the house.

"Norm replied that he didn't care about that. 'Just sign the deed over to me, and I will take care of everything else. I need my wife, not your cash.'"

Norm had made Brian an offer he couldn't refuse. He looked into Norm's eyes, and the two shook hands.

Norm didn't hesitate. "Let's go to Dan's office and sign the paperwork."

Dan Gallagher was an attorney they both had worked with in the past. Having one attorney made it easy to draw up what they wanted quickly. Within hours, they'd signed a contract, and the deal was done.

Norm drove Brian home and went back to his real estate office to finish the day, knowing he'd just saved his marriage.

Brian got into his car and drove to the dealership.

He parked in the same spot he'd used for four years, walked across the street, and took a few steps into the showroom.

The staff was surprised to see him standing there, glancing from wall to wall. He turned toward them and grinned.

"I'm back."

"What?"

"Norm sold me the business. As of tomorrow, Ferrari of Los Gatos belongs to me."

They were shocked but happy. Things hadn't been great with all the changes that had taken place over the past few months.

"We'll need to open a bank account in your name," said the office manager. "What do I deposit?"

Brian reached into his pocket and took out all the cash he had.

"Here, deposit this."

She counted the money.

"It's only $267."

"Well, that's all I have."

Thanks to the Mediterranean fruit fly, Brian's pocket cash ended up being all that he needed. Known as the Medfly, in 1981, a severe infestation was threatening California's $40-billion-a-year agricultural industry. Governor Jerry Brown authorized widespread spraying of malathion, an insecticide that shattered the fly's nervous system. The spraying also shattered the nerves of many Bay Area residents who feared the pesticide was unhealthy for children and other living things. State officials told everyone to stay indoors and keep pets inside. Bay Area residents said they shut windows and kept doors closed as soon as they heard the helicopters. One Palo Alto nurse with three children said, "It was like wartime. Like waiting for bombs to be dropped. It was something I had no control over." For days, an invisible rain of pesticide droplets fell over three counties in Silicon Valley in the war against this insect. One of the unplanned side effects of the spraying was that the bait used to carry the pesticide left tiny sticky specks on vehicles that were parked outside. And Ferrari of Los Gatos had a lot of cars uncovered on the dealership lot.

Brian filed a claim with his insurance carrier for the damage done to the cars. Like other Los Gatos residents, he didn't like his property getting sprayed on at night. Within days, he received a check from the insurance company for $48,000, and that provided the working capital he needed to get the business going again.

The guy who initially agreed to help Richard sell Ferraris back in 1976 now owned the dealership. During the next 15 years, Ferrari of Los Gatos would become the largest North American dealer and sell more Ferraris than anyone else. The dealership's success meant so much to Enzo Ferrari that he paid to bring Brian and other dealers to Italy and treated them like royalty. Eventually, the business would grow to sell more than 300 cars a year, mostly new and used Ferraris, and reach annual sales of $48 million ($124 million in 2021 dollars).

CHAPTER SEVEN

A Road Warrior

(1982)

HIS FIRST MORNING BACK AS THE DEALER, BRIAN LOCATED A DESIRABLE Ferrari for sale in Santa Monica. After buying the car, someone needed to fly to Los Angeles, pick it up, and drive it back to Los Gatos. He wondered if Rueben, the contractor working at his house, would be interested in the job. Brian liked Rueben and felt he could trust him. That might have been because of the way they met. Rueben Navarro worked for a contractor Brian had hired, but things didn't go as planned. Rueben recalled the situation.

"A friend installing siding on homes asked for my help on a large job. At the time, I had a business installing carpets. My friend said, 'Don't worry. I'll explain what to do.' The job was at Brian's house. A couple of days into the job, my friend said he was going to Oregon and wouldn't be back. He told me; the job was mine. I couldn't believe it. I went to Brian and told him someone else would need to complete the job. When Brian asked, 'Why don't you finish it?' I explained that I was a carpet installer and didn't have the equipment necessary to do this job. 'Rent whatever you need. I'll pay for everything,' Brian told me."

That was how the relationship between Rueben and Brian started. And Rueben would end up finishing the job.

Brian drove home and found Rueben cleaning up the job site and getting ready to leave.

"I have another job for you."

"What is it?"

"I have a car in Southern California that needs to be picked up. All you have to do is drive it back to Los Gatos."

"I can do that, but then I need to get back to my carpet business."

The following day, Rueben flew to Los Angeles, picked up the Ferrari, and drove it back to Los Gatos. Rueben was there the first day Brian took over Ferrari of Los Gatos and ended up being there the last day Brian operated the dealership. And he never did get back to his carpet business.

It didn't take long, and Rueben was picking up or delivering Ferraris daily. On most trips, he'd drop off one car and pick up another. Of course, there was no such thing as GPS at the time, but it didn't matter. He made so many trips to Boise, Las Vegas, Los Angeles, Phoenix, Portland, Reno, Seattle, and Tucson that he didn't even need a Thomas Bros. map book.

Eventually, the relationship between Brian and Rueben became more than just employer/employee. Rueben became the person Brian felt he could trust with anything, including his innermost feelings. Brian usually interacted with others in a strictly business manner, keeping his thoughts to himself. In the car business, you made more money that way. But when Rueben fell on tough times and needed somewhere to live, Brian and his wife Tina did something for him that not even his own family would do.

"They opened the door of their home to me, and I became part of their family," Rueben recalled. "I lived with them for years, and during that time, they never charged me anything. They even arranged a private area for me to live in their house. Who does that for you?"

Rueben was an essential part of the success of Ferrari of Los Gatos.

"On one occasion, I'd gone to pick up a new Ferrari Mondial Cabriolet in Salt Lake City. I'd never driven in snow in my life and had no idea how difficult it is. On the way back to Los Gatos, I struggled to see the road and drove slowly. At one point, the wind was blowing so hard the freeway disappeared. Everything was white except the poles marking the side of the road and the dim lights of trucks up ahead. Suddenly, I lost control of the car. I'd never lost control before and went for the brakes. Oh my God, what a mistake. The car started spinning round and round and hit a pole on the driver's side. When the car finally stopped, I was on a side ramp about 20 feet from hitting an 18-wheeler. I felt so terrible about smashing up this beautiful car; you have no idea."

Sitting on the side of the road in a blizzard, Rueben tried to catch his breath and make his heart stop pounding so fast. Then he started driving slowly, then more slowly. Finally, when he could, Rueben pulled over and called Brian to tell him the bad news.

Brian asked, "Is the car drivable?"

"Yes."

"Okay, keep going."

Rueben drove the rest of the way to Ferrari of Los Gatos, still wracked with guilt about smashing up the car. When he arrived at the dealership, he confronted Brian. "No more jobs like this for me."

Brian could be very persuasive if he needed to be. He believed anything was possible and had a no-pressure, no-problem attitude toward everything. He lived by the saying "Just Do It" years before Nike adopted this as their slogan.

He told Rueben, "Look, these cars are just a bunch of metal parts connected to four wheels. You are in control of them. I can replace any car easily but can't replace you so easily. So, if you make a mistake, learn from it, and don't do it again. But if you want to call it quits, go ahead."

The next day, Rueben asked for another trip and continued to drive many Ferraris over a total of 15 years, resulting in more incredible adventures.

Rueben did change one thing, though—he never drove a Ferrari in the snow again.

Brian was purchasing cars all over the western United States, and Rueben was picking up and delivering Ferraris, probably driving more of them than anyone else on earth—except maybe the Maranello test drivers.

Rueben's trips usually went off without a hitch. A few times, however, a standard pickup or drop-off turned into a dangerous predicament. There were times he cheated death, participated in what seemed like a scene from a gangster movie, and saw more cash than most bankers do.

"You would not believe the things I saw and the experiences I had. I was so lucky to be able to drive the fastest cars in the world."

And sometimes, he was just lucky to survive.

When Ferrari introduced the Testarossa, a 12-cylinder mid-engine model with a new body style, it became a huge success. The demand for them soared. Brian sold his factory allocation and then started buying them from other dealers. Rueben remembered the time Brian located one in Spokane, Washington, and sent him to get it.

"Boy, was that car quick."

Rueben had delivered a car in Spirit Lake, Idaho, about 20 miles north of Coeur d'Alene. The next day, he picked up the brand-new Testarossa in Spokane. Rueben felt personally responsible for every car and didn't like the idea of parking one overnight. So he decided to drive the Testarossa all night long instead of stopping along the way.

"I was driving back south to Los Gatos around midnight, driving through Oregon on Route 395, and it was dark. Thick trees lined each side of the highway. I was probably going about 60 mph, and it was hard to see either side of the road. I passed a 10-wheeler on my right as a pickup truck approached us from the opposite direction. It seemed like the two deer came out of the pickup truck's headlights. They ran across the highway and were in front of me before I knew it. I tried to avoid them, but my right front fender struck the back of the first one. Simultaneously, the left front fender hit the large one, a buck, just as he started to look up. The impact severed the buck's head, and it flew through the air, antlers and all. The 10-wheeler hit the smaller deer, sending pieces of it in every direction. When it was over, all three of us pulled over to make sure everyone was okay. Somehow the pickup truck escaped without hitting anything while deer parts covered the Testarossa and 10-wheeler. We were all pretty shaken up, but thankfully no one got hurt. Well, except for the deer; they were dead."

A mile or two down the road, Rueben pulled into a gas station and called Brian to let him know what had happened. Brian asked the same question as he did when Rueben had spun out in the snow.

"Can you drive the car?"

"Yes."

"Then what's the problem?"

Rueben yelled at him, "What do you mean what's the problem? That deer almost killed me! You have no idea."

But that was Brian. He didn't carry his emotions on his sleeves. As long as you were alive and could drive the car, everything was okay. Rueben showed up in Los Gatos the following day with deerskin and body parts covering the Testarossa. The service crew cleaned and repaired the car, erasing any trace of what happened. Only Rueben's memory of cheating death would remain.

Rueben remembered one trip that involved a car chase, a suitcase full of money, and men with ill intent. "I'd just dropped off a car and received payment in a briefcase loaded with cash. It was a Samsonite with the Ferrari logo on top. I took a taxi to my next stop to pick up a Ferrari Mondial Cabriolet and take it back to Los Gatos. The briefcase never left my hand. During the drive home, I stopped at a country crossroads store in the middle of nowhere. As I pulled up and started pumping gas, three guys in a pickup truck stared at the car. People were amazed by the cars I drove, so this was normal. I paid for the gas and bought a soda, walked back to the car, and started to leave. As I pulled out of the parking lot, the three guys in the pickup truck followed me." Rueben remembered taking money out of the briefcase to pay for the gas and soda. He wondered if they had seen the $185,000 inside. Once on the open road, the pickup truck driver accelerated, trying to pass the Ferrari and get in front. "When I saw they were trying to get in front of me, I hit the gas. Zing zoom! The Mondial Cabriolet took off in a flash. Good-bye. In a few seconds, the pickup truck lights seemed like small ants in the rearview mirror." Rueben ended the story with a laugh and a smile.

Most of the Ferraris that Rueben drove enjoyed running above the speed limit. The Daytona and Daytona Spyder had 12-cylinder engines and were like racehorses. They didn't want to be held back or driven slowly. Driving fast Ferraris regularly, Rueben watched out for the Highway Patrol, especially in California, where he did most of his driving. The unusual body styles and bright colors made the cars easy to spot, and if a police officer didn't see the Ferrari, he usually heard the engine roar.

"On another occasion, I was coming back from Southern California with a Ferrari Boxer 512 BB. You know, the 12-cylinder. In those days, the speed limit was 55 mph, and I had to be careful not to get too many speeding tickets. I was on my usual route and stopped at Denny's in Lost Hills at I-5 and Highway 46. This restaurant was my regular stop to have lunch, take a break, or put gas in the car. Highway patrol officers stopped there to take breaks as well. While they saw me plenty of times, they usually didn't say anything to me."

Until one day, when the officers got curious and asked, "Why are you here so often? What kind of job do you have?"

Rueben explained that his job involved driving to and from Los Gatos with Ferraris. When all three officers asked to see the car, Rueben walked them out to the parking lot. Excited when they saw the Ferrari, the officers asked if he'd take them for a ride. "Give me your keys and your gun," Rueben responded, "and you can take the car for a run around here by yourself." They laughed, unsure if he was serious. After all, handing over the keys to a police car, let alone a gun, was something they could not, well, should not, do. Finally, after a tad of hesitation, one of the brave officers offered Rueben the keys to his patrol car. "You want my gun too?"

"Well," Rueben started, then paused for drama, "the keys will do."

The highway patrol officer took the Ferrari for a drive and came back so happy that the other two went for a ride as well. They thanked Rueben and left but not before saying, "We hope to see you around here again."

And they did see each other again, more often than once. The officers liked Rueben, enjoyed seeing the Ferraris, and decided to give their friend some advice. "We appreciate you letting us drive these fancy cars. So, we want to return the favor with a warning. When we see a sports car on the highway, we know that, sooner or later, the driver will go over the speed limit. So, we call each other and say, 'Watch out for this car.' So, remember, if the officer that sees you speeding doesn't catch you, another one will."

Rueben already had two tickets, so this was not only sound advice but also advice he planned to take. One more, and he would have lost his license.

The advice was timely. On the next trip, it came in handy.

"I remembered the officers warning on a trip back to Los Gatos from Arizona. I always used Highway 46 to Lost Hills, where I'd get on Interstate 5 after taking a break at Denny's and getting some gas for the last part of the trip home."

On this particular night, a full moon lit the highway. And with no other cars in either direction, it was easy to see the road. What Rueben didn't see was the highway patrol car sitting at the top of an overpass. Too late to slow down, the patrol car came alive and started heading for the freeway entrance. No time to think, Rueben remembered the officer's words, and his instincts kicked in.

"I pushed the gas pedal and turned off the lights. By the time that police officer got on the freeway, I was probably a mile away. I didn't see the patrol car again until after I pulled into Denny's and parked behind the bushes at the end of the parking lot. It passed me going pretty fast." Rueben got away.

In 1989, an earthquake occurred in Los Gatos and surrounding Bay Area cities, causing Rueben to sleep at Ferrari of Los Gatos for three nights. It wasn't because he had nowhere to stay. Moments before the first pitch of the World Series baseball game between the San Francisco Giants and the Oakland Athletics, television screens all over the Bay Area went blank, and the ground shook.

"We thought it was the end of the world. We had all gathered in the showroom by the TV because it was the start of the World Series at Candlestick Park in San Francisco. When things started shaking and falling, we all made a run for the door, trying to get outside. The force of the earthquake made it difficult to move, and everyone was trying to get out at the same time. We finally all made it out of the building, the shaking stopped, and we were looking into the showroom through the openings made by several large floor-to-ceiling windows that were missing. A contractor boarded up the windows, but it took three days for them to deliver and install new glass. In the meantime, I slept in a sleeping bag on the showroom floor to make sure no one got in."

The gang at Ferrari of Los Gatos made sure there was fun in whatever they did. "If I was born again and could choose any job I wanted," Rueben said, "I doubt I could ever find one that would be that much fun."

CHAPTER EIGHT

Cut from the Same Cloth

(1971)

WILLIAM F. "BILL" HARRAH WAS A CAR COLLECTOR. AND IF IT WASN'T for Bill Harrah, Ferrari of Los Gatos might not have existed. Most people remember him as the best-known name in American gambling casinos, but he really wanted to be known as a gearhead.

In addition to running his hotel and casino empire, he was the West Coast distributor for Ferrari North America. In the 1970s, that made him responsible for deciding who became a Ferrari dealer.

Like Enzo and Brian, Bill became enthralled with the automobile growing up in Hollywood, California. His dad loved exotic cars and would take his six-year-old son along whenever he went to car shows. By the time he was a teenager, Bill had spent a lot of time checking out the cool cars cruising the scene in Hollywood. When the sports car his father bought him for his sixteenth birthday was stolen and stripped, he vowed to his sister, "One day, I will own a duplicate of every automobile the family ever had." He ended up doing that and much more.

While Enzo Ferrari used the automobile as a means to an end, Bill Harrah used classic cars to satisfy his connection with them. It was also a way for Harrah to invest the considerable profit he made from his hotel and gambling empire. From the $100-a-week Venice Beach, California, bingo game he bought from his father for $500, he built a $200 million Nevada gambling business.

Like Enzo and Brian, at times, Bill struggled. His first attempt to expand and open a gambling business in Reno failed miserably and closed in 17 days. He moved back to Venice Beach and spent the next year learning more about the Nevada gambling industry. He returned to Reno, and this time, Harrah's Plaza Tango casino was a success. The business flourished and eventually expanded into Lake Tahoe and Las Vegas. Along the way, Harrah's Corporation differentiated itself by becoming the only casino listed on the New York Stock Exchange. Some casinos allegedly skimmed profits off the top, but Bill wanted to be different. His goal was to be profitable, and he didn't mind paying taxes. After all, there were a lot of cars he wanted to buy.

Bill's love of automobiles created the world's most extensive automobile collection of more than 1,400 cars. It also created a friendship with Enzo. And as Enzo's distributor, he took a chance and gambled on two young men from Los Gatos who had a dream and big ideas. Richard and Brian reminded him of his younger self, and he had to help them out.

Differentiation facilitated the success of all three men and is part of the reason their paths crossed.

With the obscene amounts of money made by his casinos, Bill pursued his desire to own more automobiles than anyone else. Similarly, Enzo wanted to win more car races than anyone else. He used the profit from selling cars to fund racing. Enzo said he wanted to build the fastest cars on earth, and Bill said he wanted to own every vehicle's first or last model ever made. And let's not forget Brian. All he wanted was to be the number one Ferrari dealer. All these gentlemen had lofty goals, and they did everything imaginable to accomplish them.

Bill created Harrah's Automobile Collection, Inc. (HAC), and built a skilled team of individuals dedicated to buying and restoring classic automobiles. An unwavering perfectionist, he always wanted top performance from his vehicles. He was never satisfied with his cars' performance and usually tried to make them perform better by dropping larger, more powerful engines in them.

His general manager, Vern Keil, ran the day-to-day operations of Modern Classic Motors (MCM) for many years and remembered one particular vehicle. "Mr. Harrah said that driving his Ferraris back and forth from Reno to his home in Lake Tahoe was a joy in good weather, but it could be dangerous and challenging in the winter. When covered by winter snow, the road was steep and required a car with the power of a Ferrari and the ruggedness and four-wheel traction of a Jeep. So he approached Mr. Ferrari and asked him to build a four-wheel-drive F-car, no matter the cost. Ferrari flatly rejected the request."

Having a hard time accepting rejection, Bill did what any car enthusiast with unlimited funds would do. He thumbed his nose at Maranello and challenged his HAC automotive team to create the ultimate four-by-four. His team removed the engine from a 1969 Ferrari 365 GT 2+2, a car *Road and Track* magazine nicknamed the "Queen Mother of Ferraris," then clipped off the car's nose and mated both with the body of a 1969 Jeep Wagoneer.

Named the Jerrari, the car's power came from a 4.4-liter 268 CID Colombo V-12 Ferrari engine. Three twin-choke Weber 40 DFI carburetors fed the engine and produced 316 horsepower at 6,600 rpm. It rode on Monroe shocks and Michelin XVR 215/70-15 tires mounted on Cragar six-inch-wide alloy wheels.

The original Jerrari, built by Bill Harrah circa 1970. *Public domain photo, YouTube*

Performance tests of the Jerrari, conducted by *Road and Track* magazine, resulted in acceleration speeds of 0 to 60 mph in 9.4 seconds, 0 to 100 mph in 21.2 seconds, and a quarter mile in 15 seconds flat. The Jerrari posted a top speed of 125 mph, but a Harrah engineer swore it would do 130 mph. It may not sound like such a high speed by today's standards, but the tests took place more than 50 years ago.

The car became well known and easily recognized as it flew down the highway regularly between Reno and Lake Tahoe.

As Harrah's empire increased, his need for personal security increased as well. The historic Jerrari was easy to spot, and bodyguards advised him not to drive it anymore. But, still wanting the power of a Ferrari along with road-handling ability, he challenged his HAC team to build a second "Jerrari."

On the outside, Jerrari II looked like any other Jeep Wagoneer. One would realize that it was not a regular Jeep only by the Ferrari engine's rumble at a stop signal or by being left in the dust when the light turned green. The Jerrari II had standard Jeep wood paneling on the sides and a 365-horsepower Ferrari V-12 under the hood. The engine was so long that a traditional radiator would not fit. Instead, radiators were mounted on each side of the engine, making sure the motor didn't overheat, and oil coolers from a helicopter routed cold air from under the bumper.

There's usually a good story behind every classic car, and Jerrari II was no exception. Vern remembered the time a salesman came to Reno selling helicopters. "That guy assured Mr. Harrah a helicopter would allow him to get back and forth between his Reno and South Lake Tahoe properties faster. Mr. Harrah thought for a minute or two and then told the salesman he wanted to make a deal with him."

"You fly your helicopter, and I'll drive my old Jeep. If you get to Tahoe before me, I'll buy your helicopter," he told the salesman.

Harrah never owned a helicopter.

All three men seemed cut from the same cloth—inherent risk takers. And custom cars seemed to be in their DNA. Enzo built the fastest race cars in the world that won almost every race they entered. Bill did what no one had ever done before when he told his team to put a Ferrari engine

The Jerrari II, built by Bill Harrah circa 1979. *Public domain photo, Wikimedia.org*

in a Jeep. And Brian made history when he dropped a Ferrari engine into a '32 deuce coupe. Brian named his hot rod creation the Deucari.

Whether it was coincidence or fate, like identical twins, Harrah's Jerrari and Brian's Deucari had the same motor. How could two cars have the same engine?

In 1978, on a visit to MCM, Brian saw an engine sitting on a pallet. He could tell, even at a distance, it was from a Ferrari.

"What are you guys doing with that Ferrari V-12 over in the corner?"

The MCM engineer stared at it for a while and then walked over to it. "Oh yeah, we took this engine out of one of Mr. Harrah's cars years ago. It's been sitting in that corner ever since."

"Well, I might be interested in getting it out of your way if it's just collecting dust."

"You'd have to talk to Vern about that."

In 1971, Harrah had his engineers replace the 1969 Ferrari 365 GT engine in the original Jerrari with a Chevy 350 V-8 engine. With no instructions regarding what to do with the V-12 engine, they left it on a wooden pallet in the warehouse. And there it sat, unnoticed and out of everyone's way—until the day Brian saw it out of the corner of his eye.

Brian bought the engine for $3,500. At the time, this might have sounded like a high price for a used engine sitting around for years. But to Brian, it was a priceless piece for the hot rod of his dreams.

With Harrah's Ferrari engine in hand, Brian reached out to hot rod builder Dick Megugorac. Dick, known to everyone in the industry by his nickname Magoo, had built a few '29 hot rods but never a '32 and certainly never one with a Ferrari engine. Brian wanted a car with the right look and believed Magoo was the right hot-rodder for the job. He'd built hot rods with that subtle just-so stance, simple yet elegant detail work, and, perhaps most importantly, bombproof reliability. His cars drove well and could take long rides anywhere, anytime. Brian remembered surprising Magoo when the two first spoke.

"I don't think he believed me when I told him I wanted to put a Ferrari engine into a '32 highboy. I showed him a photo of the motor I'd already bought and said, 'You have a budget for whatever it takes to make it a killer; I want it as good as it can be.' He looked up from the photo and said, 'Okay.' He built a killer, and he built it exactly the way I wanted it. I loved it. And so did he."

Unlike Harrah, Brian stuck with a Ferrari theme throughout the project. Power for the highboy came from a 4.4-liter 268 CID V-12 Ferrari engine. The aluminum alloy engine had plenty of power for the 2,400-pound '32 Ford, so it was left stock. The headers were custom-made porcelainized units built by Magoo. A traditional-looking three-deuce air cleaner setup used base plates and Cal Custom filter elements and tops. Sitting underneath that were three downdraft Weber two-barrel carburetors, sometimes referred to as three ducks. The state-of-the-art suspension consisted of a Super Bell dropped axle, brake rotors, and hubs, along with VW disc brake calipers and Magoo's chrome-plated circular caliper mountings. The rear suspension consisted of Koni coil-overs with a center pivot ladder bar assembly. The rear end included a Halibrand quick-change with '56 pickup floating axles.

Brian outfitted the car with Borrani knockoff wire wheels, a Connolly leather interior, and Ferrari red paint. The wheels were 5-inchers in the front, mounted with Michelin radials, and 7½-inchers in the rear, mounted with rare 15-inch Firestone sprint car tires. Anything not painted red was either buffed aluminum or chromed. He had Magoo add a DuVall windshield and a lift-off aluminum top with a '37 Cord rear window to maintain a sleek flow from front to rear. The interior featured a Hurst shifter with a digital clock shift knob, and the dash came with a complete set of Stewart Warner gauges.

But it was the sound of the highboy that was so impressive. The combination of an open-air cockpit, the straight cuts in the quick-change, and the valve clatter and exhaust note from the Ferrari motor made the Deucari America's most beautiful-sounding roadster. And the four-throat exhaust system made sure that the Ferrari V-12 "sounds" exited to the rear.

Magoo couldn't understand why Brian never visited to check on the car's progress or make sure it was the way he wanted. Brian remembered that the car wasn't his top priority at the time. He was busy trying to build a business, raise a family, and get ahead. "I knew the guy was going to do a great job. I talked to him on the phone occasionally, and that was good enough for me. I just wanted the present from Magoo when it was done, know what I mean? I wasn't worried either. I trusted the way he did things. I don't think he understood that. I don't think others treated him that way."

When Magoo said the V-12 Ferrari was too long for the deuce coupe engine compartment, Brian's answer was simple. "Just stretch the frame, you know, the nose, about four inches from the firewall forward."

Nobody had ever done anything like this before. Other hot rod builders stretched the nose and hood where they met, making the radiator sit too high. Some hot-rodders still do that today, and the cars don't look right. "I told him just keep dropping the nose and shortening the radiator until it looks right. He said, 'Now you're talkin'.' And that's the way he did it. The reason I hired Magoo in the first place was that he knew what a car was supposed to look like when it was done."

It took about a year to complete, and Magoo took it out for its first shakedown cruise. A 1979 article by Steve Coonan in *Popular Hot Rodding* magazine starts, "'It needs more gear,' Magoo remarked as he shifted the Muncie four-speed back into third. It turned out to be the only problem with the '32 Ford, and it was a minor one."

After finishing the car, Magoo made one request to Brian.

"Would you mind if I entered the Deucari in the Oakland roadster show under your name?"

"No, I'm fine with that."

A few weeks later, Brian and his wife Tina sat in the audience at the 1979 Grand National Roadster Show in Oakland, California. Magoo parked the Deucari on a white shag carpet with gold stanchions in each corner and white rope draped between them to keep anyone from getting too close. He left one side of the hood up so that attendees could see the motor.

Brian didn't expect to win anything, but he sure felt proud to have his car sitting next to others that had come from as far away as Europe to enter the contest. It also pleased him to see Magoo getting congratulated for the great job he'd done.

When they got to the roadster class, he sat upright and paid more attention, even though he didn't expect to hear his name. The show announcer went through third place, second place, and then the first-place winner. They were all someone else, which is what Brian expected anyhow. At this point, he thought, *I may not have won anything, but I sure am having a good time.*

"Honestly, I didn't give a shit. It was great having Tina there and having the chance to get your name on that eight-foot perpetual trophy. It's the one your name stays on forever, and you go down in infamy."

Thinking the roadster section was over, Brian and Tina got up to leave. As they did, the announcer came back on. "And, the winner of the 1979 America's Most Beautiful Roadster award is Brian Burnett with his '32 Roadster, the Deucari."

The Deucari, built by Dick "Magoo" Megugorac for Brian Burnett, circa 1979. *Personal photo Brian Burnett*

Surprised and excited, Brian and Magoo accepted the award together, and both of their lives changed. Magoo became instantly famous, and his shop got so busy that he was turning down new projects. Within a month, Brian was drag racing the Deucari, and car enthusiasts couldn't believe it. Other show winners were garaged and transported on trailers or car haulers. Many trophy cars' wheels never touched anything but showroom floors. Once again, Brian differentiated himself by driving and racing the Deucari. That alone made the car different than any other America's Most Beautiful Roadster–winning hot rod. That Deucari became known as the show car that got driven.

Coonan's 1979 article ended with, "After receiving top awards in all the major West Coast car shows, including winning the Oakland Most Beautiful Roadster trophy, Brian now plans to enjoy the car to its fullest, and that means plenty of road miles. The sight and sound combination of Ferrari V-12 growl, Muncie and Halibrand whine, and that gleaming red lacquer all wrapped up in the classic highboy silhouette is something that really can't be missed."

And for the guy who didn't care if he won or not, there is an eight-foot trophy sitting in a museum that says, "For the Deucari, a highboy Deuce powered by a Ferrari V-12, built for Brian Burnett—1979." The trophy will be there forever.

Years later, Jonnie King, a professional hot rod radio broadcaster, interviewed Magoo at the Darryl Stoddard National Rod and Custom Car Hall of Fame Museum in Afton, Oklahoma. Jonnie wanted to know about the most challenging car Magoo had ever built.

"With all the roadsters and cars that you screwed together over the years, were there any that gave you a hard time?" asked Jonnie.

Magoo didn't hesitate. "Well, you gotta remember we were the first ones to put a Ferrari in a '32. A Ferrari dealer came to me and said he wanted to put a Ferrari engine in this '32. I said, a Ferrari engine? The idea was outrageous, and I thought he was kidding. He said, 'Yes, I want you to go to Hollywood and pick up the motor I already bought. I want a '32 roadster with a Ferrari in it.' I agreed and started planning and engineering the car. He named it the Deucari.

America's Most Beautiful Roadster (AMBR) Perpetual Trophy, Oakland Roadster Show. *Personal photo Brian Burnett*

"The biggest thing was you had to stretch it, adapt an American four-speed transmission to the Ferrari engine, which took a lot of machining and time, and put Ferrari wheels on it."

"Who did you build the Deucari for, and how long did it take?"

"I built it for Brian Burnett, a Ferrari dealer in the Bay Area. I guess it took us a pretty good part of a year to finish it. But that car was one of the best-running cars I ever had."

The Deucari proved it was more than just a show queen. Most hot rods seen at shows never had their tires touch the street. Not so for the Deucari. Brian drove it from Los Gatos to Memphis for the 1980 Street Rod Nationals and took it for a few passes down the dragstrip. The car turned in a best elapsed time of 13.01 seconds at 105 mph. It also

The crowd watches as the Deucari gets ready to speed down the drag strip in Fremont, California. *Personal photo Brian Burnett*

spent some time on the Fremont drag strip in Northern California. Hot rod enthusiasts loved the fact that the car was being driven and raced, increasing its popularity immensely.

The Deucari and both Jerraris are still around today. The Deucari is privately owned and hangs out in Southern California. The original Jerrari has done its rounds on the auction circuit, including an eBay sale in 2008. In the summer of 2021, it appeared for sale in *Classic Driver* magazine. The listing states "price on request." The Jerrari II isn't for sale. It's a permanent resident of the National Automobile Museum in Reno, Nevada.

Like the Deucari, Ferrari of Los Gatos was firing on all cylinders, and the good times seemed as though they'd never end.

CHAPTER NINE

Five Bags

(1988)

IN HIS 1962 AUTOBIOGRAPHY, ENZO FERRARI SAID MOST CUSTOMERS fell into one of three categories: the sportsman, the 50-year-old, or the exhibitionist. However, at Ferrari of Los Gatos, there was at least one other category.

People from all walks of life came through the showroom doors of the dealership, many just to look. It was a fun place to hang out. In addition to new and used Ferraris, there were also hot rods and other classic cars. In 1988, when muscle cars became popular for the second time around, there were usually one or two of those on the lot as well.

The dealership became well known to many car enthusiasts and caught the attention of some with unusual sources of income. A never-ending stream of peculiar characters came to visit Ferrari of Los Gatos, some with surprising requests.

One day, a GMC motor home drove up and parked in front of the lot. Four guys wearing bell-bottom blue jeans, one with an open-collared shirt and three in T-shirts, stepped out, looked around, and walked onto the dealership lot. In the 1980s, just a glance at a group like this told you what they did for a living.

The gentleman in the open-collared shirt walked into the showroom, approached the nearest employee, and said, "Who's Brian Burnett?" The salesman pointed toward the back office.

Brian and his friend Steve, a retired police officer and narcotics agent, had watched the group exit the car from his office. Brian liked having Steve around. Not only was he a good friend, but he knew how to take care of himself. Sometimes strange people came into the dealership, and it was nice to have him around to watch over things. Steve always packed a gun just in case.

"I'm Brian Burnett, what can I do for you?" he said, reaching out to shake the visitor's hand.

"My name is Jake, and I'd like to buy that orange Roadrunner you have out on the lot." He didn't take Brian's hand as he spoke but pointed outside instead. "A friend of mine said if anyone could meet my terms and conditions, it would be you."

When the group first walked in, Steve told Brian to be careful. From prior police work, Steve's instinct felt like the group might be in an illegal line of work.

The orange 1969 Plymouth Roadrunner Hemi was a classic muscle car that had been raced. It still had slick racing tires on the rear and could do the quarter mile in 10 seconds or less. Brian quoted about $20,000 above the car's minimum price just to see if Jake was for real.

"Sure, that car will cost you $75,000 plus tax and license. If that works, I'll listen to the other conditions."

Without hesitation or negotiation, Jake responded, "That will be no problem as long as you can deliver it up to my house and meet my terms."

"And what might they be?"

Jake said he had to have the car by high noon the next day without explaining why. He also said Brian would need to deliver it personally.

"I'd like to show you my place and pay you when you get up there."

Brian said he usually sent his crew out to deliver cars and wasn't sure he'd be able to do it himself. "You've got 75,000 reasons to make this delivery yourself, Brian," Jake responded.

Brian didn't have to think too long. The price had an extra $20,000 profit, he wanted to move it off the lot, and he sensed that Jake wasn't someone who accepted no for an answer.

"Okay, we got us a deal. Now how would you like to handle the payment?"

At this point, Jake asked to speak in private. They walked into Brian's office, and he closed the door. "Now Mr. Burnett," Jake said, "in my line of work, we don't like to disclose too much about our business. Everything we buy or sell is a cash transaction, no questions asked. Is that going to be a problem?"

"No, sir," Brian replied. "As long as I'm paid in full upon delivery of the vehicle, I have no problem with an all-cash payment." Jake gave Brian a cash deposit to cover the sales tax and license fees and assured him the $75,000 balance would be taken care of at his home the next day. This time, Jake reached out his hand to shake Brian's, said good-bye, and walked back to the motor home, where his associates stood waiting.

Ferrari of Los Gatos owned a Chevrolet flatbed hauler to move cars around and occasionally deliver them locally. Brian told his service team to get the car ready to be delivered tomorrow and load it up on the hauler. Next, he instructed his office staff to prepare paperwork for an all-cash transaction. The sales documents had to be finished by the next morning to make sure Brian could meet the mysterious high-noon delivery deadline.

Around 11 a.m. Friday, the car sat securely on the hauler. To feel safe, Brian decided to bring his friend Steve along. They had instructions on how to get to the house but no actual address. Brian and Steve jumped in the truck, drove out to the Nimitz Highway 17, and headed west up the mountain toward Santa Cruz.

As they drove toward the summit, Steve told Brian to turn just before the Cloud 9 restaurant after the three tall pine trees. Brian turned onto a windy road and had to drive slowly, but it gave them enough time to make sure they were going the right way. The delivery instructions contained no street names, just landmark hints on how to find the right roads.

"Brian, turn right at the two fallen trees," said Steve, "and then turn left at the road that seems more like a U-turn than a left turn. You'll know which one it is by all the scrapes on the pavement made by trucks."

After the last turn, they found themselves in the middle of nowhere. Even though it was late morning, the thick trees kept the road shaded and in the dark. It wasn't easy to see.

"Shit, did you see that?" Brian asked, a tad of fear in his voice.

"No, what?"

"I swear I saw someone in the bushes holding something up. Right back there. You didn't see it?"

"Nah, I saw nothing. Just some shadows. Maybe you're seeing things?" Steve laughed.

"Ha ha. Very funny. Unlike you, I don't have a gun to protect myself."

"Don't worry, I'll protect you with that gun, too," Steve giggled.

"Right."

The narrow road and the shadows made Brian nervous, and he continued to drive very slowly. He kept glancing at his watch, worried that they might not make it by high noon.

"Shit!" Steve said.

"What?"

"Someone is leaning against that tree back there!"

"I can't see anything," Brian said, looking back toward the tree. "Must have been shadows." This time, he was the one who giggled as he turned to look back.

Turning his eyes back to the road, he barely had time to react. Brian hit the brakes so hard that Steve slid into the dashboard as the truck came to an abrupt stop, just in time to avoid a man five yards in front of them. The man was holding a gun.

"That's an Uzi," Steve said as he sat back up.

The man stepped aside.

"Well, as long as he's not shooting at us, let's keep going," Brian said. For the next half mile, they saw an armed guard every couple hundred yards. They were sitting on rocks, leaning on trees, and sometimes perched on the branch of a tree. It was evident that if you weren't supposed to be there, you weren't getting in.

Brian and Steve were getting anxious—it was close to high noon, delivery time. Finally, reaching the end of the road, the hauler came to a gate and a long gravel driveway. Guards checked the truck inside and out while Brian and Steve sat motionless. Once the guards seemed satisfied, one of them signaled to a camera mounted on a pole. The gates opened slowly, and the guard motioned Brian to move ahead. Once inside, the gates closed quickly behind Brian and Steve.

"Looks like no one talks around here."

"Just follow whatever they motion us to do," instructed Steve. "We'll be outta here in no time."

Driving up the steep incline, they reached a large circular drive in front of a big log house. It seemed like twenty people came out of the house to greet them. Most of the group were under 30 and showed visible excitement when they saw the car on the truck. Brian climbed onto the flatbed, got into the car, and started it up. The muscle car had no mufflers, and when the group heard the engine roar, they cheered and clapped. They loved it.

The commotion summoned Jake outside, too. He was smiling, "Come on in guys; we're just getting ready to eat lunch."

Brian and Steve did not feel like socializing with someone guarded by a small army and tried to make excuses.

"Nonsense, we have to finish our business," Jake insisted. "If you want to get paid, you must join us for lunch, have a few drinks, and join us for our movie. We watch *The Long Riders* at 2 p.m. every day in our theater."

"Every day?" questioned Brian.

"Most of my men work the night shift," Jake replied with a smile. "We want you to hang around and watch the movie with us."

Brian decided they had no choice. If he wanted to see his money, they'd better have lunch and watch the movie. The group had a long lunch together, and when no one could eat any more, they moved to another room called the theater. In that room was the most massive couch Brian had ever seen—a U-shaped sectional that could hold about 25 people. Everyone took a seat, and as they were talking, an eight-foot screen rolled down from the ceiling, and a large projector showed the movie on it.

The Long Riders is a 1980 movie about the most notorious American bandits of the nineteenth century, the Jesse James/Cole Younger gang. In the film, real-life actor brothers starred as the James, Younger, Ford, and Miller brothers. Actors David, Keith, and Robert Carradine played the Younger brothers, James and Stacy Keach played Jesse and Frank James, Dennis and Randy Quaid played the Miller brothers, and Christopher and Nicholas Guest played the Ford brothers.

Director Walter Hill claimed the movie was as close to the truth as legends can ever be. As the brothers rob and revel throughout the West, pursued by bumbling lawmen, viewers felt they were actually in the unpredictable, unconventional, raw America of the 1870s.

Brian had seen the movie before, and it wasn't one of his favorites. Watching it, however, seemed like the right thing to do under the circumstances.

Throughout the movie, Jake and his entourage would cheer. They acted like it was the first time they ever saw the movie, even though it played on schedule at 2 p.m. every day.

During the movie, Jake's entourage smoked wacky tobacky the size of a football, causing them to laugh uncontrollably at times. At the beginning of the film, Brian and Steve couldn't wait for it to end, but the cheering and the laughing helped make the movie more enjoyable. They had burritos toward the end of the film, and those were a big hit. It was a long afternoon, but everyone, including Brian and Steve, had a good time.

"All the world likes an outlaw. For some damn reason, they remember 'em."
—Jesse James. *United Archives GmbH/Alamy Stock Photo*

"Well, it's time for us to go," Brian said after the movie ended. "We need to get back over the hill. We'll go outside and unload the car and drive the hauler back to the dealership."

Before Brian took a step, Jake asked, "Now Brian, just how much did you say that car was gonna cost me?"

A bit worried that Jake might try to bargain for a lower price or, worse yet, that he'd figured out there was some extra profit in the deal, he responded quickly, "Seventy-five thousand."

Turning toward one of his associates, Jake ordered, "Bring 'em three bags."

Oh boy, what was Jake going to do, give him bags of drugs?

Sensing the concern on Brian's face, Jake smiled and explained, "We keep 25 large in each bag." Although that seemed somewhat reassuring, Brian couldn't wait to unload the car and get out of there.

Jake's associates handed Brian three heavy-duty paper bags stapled closed.

"Want to count it?"

"That's not necessary. We trust you," Brian said. The first few times Brian was paid with cash, he had his office staff count it to make sure it was right. It turned out that every time, there was more money than needed, never less. When Brian returned the overage, he'd usually hear, "Oh man, geez, I'm sorry. Thank you so much." When he asked others why there was always extra cash, he found out his customers were testing him to see if he could be trusted. In this line of business, trust could be the difference between life and death.

At last, they had their money and were ready to unload the car and head for home. As they walked out the door to unload the car, Jake said, "Hold on a second. I think you better just leave that car right up there on that truck."

Brian began thinking the worst. Steve raised his hand slightly, signaling Brian to stay calm. As a retired police officer, he'd been in similar situations before.

"I like that truck, Brian, and I might just need it to haul my car around. What would it take for the hauler also?"

The Chevrolet sloped-back hauler had shiny chrome wheels, and Brian's service crew kept it clean and detailed to perfection at all times. Ferrari of Los Gatos was painted on each side, giving the hauler a unique look.

"I don't want to sell the hauler," Brian said. "We use it almost every day."

"Well, if you could get enough to buy another one, what would it take just to leave the hauler with the roadrunner on it?"

Without hesitation, Brian responded, "Two bags."

Everyone started laughing, and Jake sent his man downstairs for some more money.

Brian took the bags and walked out front with them. He turned to Steve and said, "Now we need to figure out how to get home."

"Oh no, no, one of my boys will take you home," Jake said and shook Brian's hand. "Thank you. It's been a lot of fun."

Ferrari of Los Gatos sloped-back hauler. *Personal photo Brian Burnett*

Brian and Steve jumped into the car and took off with Jake's man, happy to be headed back to Ferrari of Los Gatos. Some people might feel anxious riding in a stranger's car with five bags totaling $125,000 cash on the seat next to them. But after what Brian and Steve had been through that afternoon, the ride home seemed almost relaxing.

The roadrunner stayed in the Santa Cruz Mountains for a couple of years until one day Jake decided he wanted to sell it back to Ferrari of Los Gatos. When Brian checked the odometer, he realized the car had not been driven much at all. In fact, it looked like it had only been driven up and down Jake's long driveway a few times.

Brian bought the roadrunner from Jake and sold it to a car enthusiast in Texas who wanted to street race it.

And that was the last he ever heard of the car or the customer who insisted on a cash transaction, no questions asked.

Chapter Ten

Maranello

(1982–1987)

Enzo Ferrari appreciated what Brian and the other dealers did to create and grow the North American market for his cars. After all, money from car sales allowed him to continue achieving his most important goals in life—speed and victory. To show his appreciation, Enzo invited Brian and other dealers to visit the Maranello factory and spend some time getting to know his Italian homeland.

But he valued and appreciated something else about the dealers as well. Like himself, they loved cars. The love of cars created a passion day in and day out. It became the catalyst to their success. And the love was shared by their customers. Whether they were rich or not, men or women, cops, dads, criminals, or upstanding citizens, they all shared a passion for the machine. By 1982, annual sales of Ferraris in North America had reached 1,000, an increase of five times since Ferrari of Los Gatos opened in 1976.

When asked about that trip, Brian became visibly excited.

"The trips to Italy were unequaled by anything else during my time as a Ferrari dealer."

Brian recalled how special the trips were. The first trip held a special place in his memory.

"I'll never forget that first trip to Italy. It had been an outstanding year for Ferrari, and Enzo decided to invite the North American dealers to visit Italy. The trip was exclusive, dealers with wives or girlfriends only. Ferrari provided Alitalia coach-class plane tickets, although most dealers upgraded to business class at their own expense. My wife Tina and I met the other dealers in Chicago the day before, and several of us stayed at the same hotel. We had dinner together and enjoyed trying to imagine what we'd be doing on the trip.

"The next day we boarded a 747 jet to London and took over the business-class section. The Alitalia attendants laid out a table of cheeses, little meats, and wine. All this wine! I don't know if Ferrari was paying for that or what, but it was terrific. Dealers that sat in coach came up front after takeoff and partied with the rest of us."

In a 747, the pilot cockpit and first-class cabin are upstairs, with business class downstairs in the front of the plane. The pilots probably had to tilt the aircraft's nose up since the group of Ferrari dealers stayed in business class for the entire flight.

"Halfway through the flight, guitarist and singer-songwriter Kenny Loggins and his wife Eva came downstairs and asked if they could join the party. Of course, we were delighted to have them join us. I don't even know if he had a Ferrari or not. I don't think anybody asked him. I don't think anybody cared."

The 10-hour flight gave everyone time to meet face-to-face and get to know each other. Most of the other dealers recognized Brian's voice because he had called to buy cars many times. "The other dealers, most of them older and more experienced than I, were nice to me. They called me the young kid from California."

After arriving in Italy and getting settled in their hotel, Brian and Tina tried to sleep. But, unfortunately, sleeping didn't come easy after the party, the jet lag, and the excitement of the trip.

The next day started too early. But the Italian breakfast served by the hotel helped to open everyone's eyes. After all, food is one of the reasons to travel to Italy. Every meal in Italy includes bread—and usually lots of it. Breakfast was no exception. Bread, butter, and jam make up probably the most traditional part of the meal. Then there are the pastries: Fette Biscottate (breakfast galettes), Cornetto (croissants), and Saccottino and Bauletto (pastries filled with chocolate, custard cream, or jam) that can please anyone's sweet tooth. An Italian biscotti (dunkable breakfast biscuit) and a caffé, cappuccino, or latte macchiato complete breakfast.

After indulging in the beautiful Italian breakfast, two Fiat buses took the dealers to the factory.

Brian remembered feeling strange after they arrived. "Standing in the Maranello factory hallway, we could tell something special was going on. Security people were standing around everywhere. The group was escorted into a large room with only one table and one unoccupied chair. A few moments later, the room went silent as Enzo Ferrari walked in. He wore a long beige coat and dark black sunglasses."

Enzo had not been seen in public without sunglasses since 1956, when his 24-year-old son Dino died. Whether it was Dino's death or that Enzo hated the flash and camera lights at press conferences and photo shoots, he kept the sunglasses on constantly, even indoors.

The expressionless white-haired gentleman sitting at the table spoke very little. As most Italians do, he gestured by lifting and spreading his hands open to do his speaking. As his hands shifted direction around the room, they said welcome and thank you. He didn't need to say a word.

Enzo Ferrari with the North American dealers, 1982. *Personal photo Brian Burnett*

Then Enzo nodded his head and started inviting each dealer to come forward, one by one. He called each dealer's name in English but with a heavy Italian accent and announced their dealership location.

Brian remembered feeling like he was about to meet the pope or the king of a country. "To be in the presence of this man was awe-inspiring. He'd built the greatest automobile dynasty in the world, one that would win more than 4,000 races and 13 world championships, and we all respected him for that. He also provided a product for us to sell that helped us create successful businesses. And for that, we were very grateful."

Enzo showed his respect to the North American dealers by shaking their hands, saying a few words in broken English, and giving them an autographed copy of *Auto Piloti*, the book he'd written about his time as a race car driver.

In their book *The Ferrari Phenomenon*, authors Matt Stone and Luca Dal Monte quoted Nikki Lauda, a Ferrari Formula One Grand Prix world champion driver. "Enzo was a tough cookie and demanded a lot from his team, but he was an Italian with a big heart. If he respected you, he was still hard to deal with, but at the same time, you knew that he liked you."

They also quoted Ferrari Formula One racing driver Mario Andretti explaining why he and his brother Aldo wanted to race. "Ferrari," was his answer. "If motor racing caught your imagination as an Italian kid, it was because of the Ferrari magic. It remained that way for me, and it captured the imagination of the rest of the world. So, if you talk about Ferrari, and I don't care where you are, what corner of the planet you are in, people will know what you're talking about."

When Brian heard Enzo call his name, he thought about Jim Kimberly and his red 375 MM, the first Ferrari he'd seen or heard with his dad some 30 years earlier. Now he was about to shake hands with its creator.

Enzo kept Brian at the table a little longer than the other dealers, and it wasn't because he sold more cars. It was because of the Deucari, a 1932 Ford deuce Brian had customized with a Ferrari engine. The resulting hot rod had Ferrari paint, upholstery, and wheels. Enzo opened a book to a picture of the Deucari and asked in broken English, "You make this one?" When Brian said yes, Enzo smiled, nodded his approval, and shook Brian's hand a second time.

"Enzo made my childhood dream come true that day. Getting a compliment on the Deucari from him made it extra special."

After the meeting, Ferrari provided a sit-down lunch in the factory courtyard, where a vehicle was hidden under a red cloth. During lunch, the red cover came off, revealing the 1982 Ferrari Mondial Quattro-valvole. The Mondial was a welcome addition to the line. It was still a rear-engine, transverse, 90-degree V-8, but Ferrari engineers opted for the four-valve-per-cylinder engine to make it more of a mainstream sports car. The Mondial unveiling to the dealers took place even before the public had seen it.

After the factory tour, Ferrari took the dealers to Fiorano, the test track that usually did not have outside visitors. They brought out test drivers to run two Formula One (F1) cars around the track. The dealers

Ferrari unveils the 1982 Ferrari Mondial Quattrovalvole to North American dealers in Maranello. *Personal photo Brian Burnett*

watched the cars roar by and were allowed to view them up close when they finished.

"We couldn't ride in the F1 cars since they only had one seat but got to ride in 1982 model 308 Ferraris driven by the test drivers. The 308 models had seats for a driver and a passenger. It was an experience beyond anything one could imagine. You were always worried that something terrible would happen because the driver would be talking to you with his hands like Italians do—while driving!" Brian remembered grasping the door handle (or anything in reach) so tightly that his knuckles turned white. "You'd be sitting there, thinking, 'He's not holding on to the steering wheel!' Then, steering with their knees, they'd head into corners, going 90 miles per hour, scaring the crap out of you. I mean, seriously, I am a pretty good driver, but these Ferrari guys are just in another stratosphere."

The first day in Maranello had been epic for the dealers, and there was more to come. The dealer's group totaled about 100, and Ferrari provided about 20 staff to travel with them. Brian remembered it took two buses to carry everyone to each destination.

"We got on those buses every morning, and they took us everywhere. We stayed at the hotel Fini in Maranello, the old one right downtown. And the bartender at the hotel was one of the coolest Italians I ever met. He'd stay up until four or five in the morning if we wanted him to. The Hollywood dealer loved Ouzo, a Greek liquor, while the rest of us enjoyed Italian grappa. By the time we checked out, I'm sure the hotel had run out of both."

Every day was a new adventure on those buses. One day it was Pompeii, the next Rome. "One day, we did a tour to see so many statues that they all started looking the same to me. I wasn't that interested in statues, but we did it all. On every bus trip, the dealers would have some wine or other beverages, and we'd drink on the bus and get so blasted by the time we got anywhere. Steve Harris, the Salt Lake City dealer, would always bring two bottles of limoncello on the bus with him—that's Italian lemon vodka. On one trip, Steve runs out of limoncello. Since the bus is in traffic, he goes up and tells the bus driver, 'I'm gonna run up the street here until I find someplace to buy more limoncello. Just keep an eye out and don't pass me up.' Steve disappeared up the street, and a block or two later comes running back to the bus and gets on with two bottles. I mean, these people were crazy, you know."

In the second week of this trip, Ferrari moved the dealers to Florence, the capital of Tuscany and the most popular city in that region. The drive gave the dealers a one-hour-and-45-minute breathtaking display of the Tuscan countryside.

The city of Florence, described as an "open-air museum," is recognized worldwide as one of the top cities for art and architecture with its many historic buildings, monuments, and rich museums. The dealers stayed at a hotel just steps from the L-shaped square, Piazza della Signoria. Located in front of the Palazzo Vecchio and gateway to the Uffizi Gallery, the Piazza sits at the center of Florentine culture, packed with Florentines and tourists. The Uffizi Gallery is one of the oldest and most famous art museums. It includes works of art from the thirteenth to eighteenth centuries by Michelangelo, Leonardo da Vinci, and Raffaello and the most extensive Botticelli collection. It was a short walk from the hotel to browse the boutiques along the Ponte Vecchio, have an espresso at a local café, and enjoy the best Florence had to offer.

"In Florence, we'd get into groups and walk the city together. On this first trip, we all got to know each other pretty well. We enjoyed doing things together, and the Ferrari people took good care of us. Ferrari didn't seem to be on a budget. Everything on these trips was first class, regardless of the cost."

The trips that followed were different. Instead of spending time near the factory in Maranello, the dealers stayed at luxury resorts and went on tours of famous sights throughout Italy. Enzo continually showed his appreciation by putting the dealers in luxurious surroundings wherever they went. "On one trip, they took us to Positano, the exclusive holiday resort town on the Amalfi Coast, and rented an entire hotel for our group."

Positano was a relatively poor fishing village during the first half of the twentieth century that began attracting tourists after *Harper's Bazaar* magazine published a John Steinbeck article in May 1953 titled "Positano Bites Deep." In it, Steinbeck wrote, "It is a dream place that isn't quite real when you are there and becomes beckoningly real after you have gone." The beach and shopping along the quaint streets seem to be the main attractions. And even though the Spiaggia Grande beach is one of the largest on the Amalfi Coast, the tips of umbrellas seem to touch each other, making it difficult to find an open space. Positano attracts an elite group of travelers, primarily intellectuals, artists, and celebrities. The North American dealers who sold the most prestigious car in the world fit in just fine.

It's difficult not to purchase souvenirs from Positano. For example, the shops claim to offer the most beautiful sandals in the world. A customer chooses the style and decorations, a craftsperson measures their foot, and within about half an hour, a pair of custom sandals is ready. Clothing and other souvenirs are hard to pass up as well. New York dealer Steven Kessler said, "I had to buy a suitcase to bring home the keepsakes from Positano."

Another time, the dealers stayed at the Villa d'Este on Lake Como, one of the top hotels in the world. In 2009, *Forbes* magazine ranked it the best hotel in the world. An average room runs $1,214 a night, while the suites command $4,250 a night. Again, Ferrari spared no expense to make sure the North American dealers had accommodations worthy of royalty.

One evening, the dealers boarded a boat that cruised to Isola Comacina. As they approached the island, it looked like they were going to a small castle. It turned out to be the famous restaurant that opened in 1948, Locanda dell'Isola Comacina. The dealers were lavished with incredible food and remarkable wine and participated in a traditional activity at the end of the evening. Every night, the maître d' created a punch beverage in a large bowl onstage and revealed who the restaurant staff had voted as the prettiest woman in the audience. She would be brought up onstage to have the honor of receiving the first sip of the punch. Brian recalled the evening. "I figured they'd pick my wife Tina, and sure enough, they did. They called her up on stage, everyone clapped, and she got the first taste of the punch. They enjoy life so much in Italy. It's almost unbelievable." Italian traditions get handed down over the years, and that night was no exception. "It might sound like nothing in

Sandal shop in Positano. *Personal photo Brian Burnett*

retrospect, but all of us were having so much fun, getting along so well, and building relationships with each other. I became terrific friends with the other dealers."

Time after time, the dealers were surprised by what Ferrari planned for them. Brian felt bonded with the other dealers and believed it was part of what made them more successful when they returned home.

"These activities tied us together in a special way, creating memories to last a lifetime. I can't remember all my relatives' names, but I can recall most of my fellow dealers' names. We went to so many cool places, like restaurants with no signs on the door frequented by wealthy locals. The entrance would be in an alley, you'd go in, and the food was, well, there just wasn't any way you were going to get a bad meal in Italy. The wine would come out in a pitcher. Nobody ordered it, and it wasn't in some special bottle with a cork to sniff. Yet it tasted as good as any high-priced wine I'd ever had. There was nothing bad! That's why I loved Italy so much. These trips were wonderful, so full of life, and the people we met were kind and gracious."

The dealers usually flew back to the United States from London. However, on one trip, the dealers experienced an unforgettable ride from Venice to London on the Venice Simplon-Orient-Express.

The original Orient Express made its final run from Paris to Istanbul on May 20, 1977. It seemed the train that carried anybody who was anybody to the edges of the Orient since 1883 was gone for good. But at a Sotheby's auction later that year, American shipping container businessman James B. Sherwood purchased two original Orient Express carriages. He'd just bought the Hotel Cipriani in Venice and planned to use the train cars to connect from his London office to his new property. Over the next five years and $31 million later, he purchased 16 more original carriages and restored them as close as possible to their original state. Finally, in the spring of 1982, the revived Orient Express, named the Venice Simplon-Orient-Express, rolled out of Victoria Station en route to Venice.

The Venice Simplon-Orient-Express remains a "hidden jewel" that is still running today, complete with white-gloved stewards in replicated uniforms waving folks aboard to enjoy lavishly decorated surroundings and the best in "culinary sophistication." An overnight passage from London to Venice has a price tag between $5,000 and $30,000. But hey, meals are included. The grand suite, a rosewood and damask sleeping carriage with a living room, costs about $18,000, although it does have complimentary champagne.

Brian recalled the end of that trip with unbridled excitement.

"At the end of one trip, Ferrari told us we are going from Venice to London on the Orient Express. Our group would be taking over the entire train that night, all 18 cars. We had to dress for dinner, and that meant I had to buy a tuxedo. It was worth it. The walk from our stateroom to the dining car took us along walls of gorgeous inlaid wood. Arriving at our dining car, we found comfortable chairs, white linen tablecloths, and a place setting that resembled a state dinner for royalty. The food served rivaled a Michelin three-star restaurant."

And the experience didn't end after dinner.

"After dinner, we moved to the lounge car, where the Ferrari America manager played the piano and sang songs for our listening and dancing pleasure. We enjoyed the music while riding through the Swiss Alps. It was just breathtaking. When we got to the English Channel, we switched to a day train to get to London and our flight back to the states. It was quite a letdown riding on a regular train, and it was depressing to fly home."

Brian and Tina ready to board the Venice Simplon-Orient-Express. *Personal photo Brian Burnett*

The trips continued every two or three years throughout the 1980s, and sometimes they took the dealers to destinations other than Italy.

"They took us to many places and didn't skimp on anything. After two trips to Italy, Ferrari changed direction, flying the dealers to San Francisco, where they sailed under the Golden Gate Bridge on a cruise ship heading north to Alaska. Once we arrived in Alaska, the ship took us back to the inland waterways. I remember they had skeet shooting on the ship, but the fog was so bad the skeet would disappear immediately. It didn't matter; we all enjoyed just shooting the guns."

And then there was the year Ferrari flew the dealers back on the Concorde supersonic airliner. "Our group was split in half because the airline could only take 50 of us per day. In those days, there were people on the Concorde that had standing reservations for years in advance. Others commuted from New York to Europe two or three times a week. The Concorde was one of the wildest experiences I've ever had. During the flight, you could see the curvature of the Earth out the window. The food was to die for. Ferrari was good to the North American dealers."

However, in 1988, Enzo died, and things changed. The dealer trips changed—they were no longer exclusive and lost their excitement. Ferrari became a company in disarray. Their inventory of unsold cars was the highest ever, and no one seemed to be in charge. In their book *The Ferrari Phenomenon*, Stone and Dal Monte wrote, "Three years after the death of Enzo Ferrari, his legendary company was in shambles. In Formula One, the Prancing Horse was at an all-time low. The road car lineup wasn't in much better shape. The 348 was not the Berlinetta Enzo Ferrari had wanted, and the courtyards in Maranello were filled with unsold Mondials. The only model selling half well was the 412, a car that was six years old. The management running the company after the passing of the founder had not been able to continue in the direction he mandated. Times were tough and a solution needed to be found—quickly."

After winning eight world championships under Enzo, it would be 12 years before Ferrari would win again. It took three years for the controlling shareholder, Fiat, to put someone in charge and start making changes.

Unfortunately, the changes would not be good for the North American dealers. Like Camelot, what once had seemed so perfect was about to come to an end.

CHAPTER ELEVEN

Customers

(1976–1993)

TUCKED IN BETWEEN SILICON VALLEY AND THE PACIFIC OCEAN SIT the Santa Cruz Mountains. The southern half of the mountain range, referred to as Sierra Azul, is cut in half by State Route 17, a highway with history.

In 1934, California designated the highway as State Route 13 and described it as "Santa Cruz to Junction US 101 at San Rafael, via San Jose." In 1940, it was rerouted and renamed State Route 17, which locals converted to "Highway 17." It consisted of three lanes with a combination of sharp turns, blind curves, and dense traffic. It became known as one of the most dangerous roads in California. The middle lane was known as the suicide lane because drivers could use it to pass other cars going either direction. As the only path to the ocean from Silicon Valley, the crowded highway cut right through the sleepy little town of Los Gatos. Drivers didn't stop unless they needed gas.

In 1976, things changed.

The population of Los Gatos had reached 25,000, and a new four-lane freeway transported cars loaded with families past the town every weekend. News of the dealership had spread, and Los Gatos became known as "the town with the Ferraris." Ferrari of Los Gatos became a popular destination point rather quickly. On weekend family outings, dads used any excuse to detour the family to that magical corner on Pageant Way and East Main Street, hoping to see some fantastic cars. One favorite was, "I need to stop and check the oil and water before we drive over the hill. I wouldn't want the car to overheat or conk out." As the car

99

slowly passed the Ferrari dealership, a simple "Wow, check out those cool cars, let's take a quick look" would usually work.

There's no question that Ferrari of Los Gatos helped improve the town's economy while boosting local businesses. Of course, not every visitor bought a Ferrari, but many had a cup of coffee, ate a meal, or picked up something from one of the nearby boutique shops. Restaurant and retail store owners reminisce of those days, and some claim their families succeeded because of all the customers Ferrari of Los Gatos brought to town. People told Brian they moved to Los Gatos because of his dealership. They came to see the cool cars they'd heard were in Los Gatos and ended up falling in love with the city.

Another boost to the popularity of Los Gatos and its very own Ferrari dealer was the annual car show in Monterey, California. Monterey Car Week, considered among the best automotive shows in America, would have up to 100,000 car enthusiasts in attendance. No matter which Northern California airport the international travelers would use, they'd pass Los Gatos on their way to Monterey. Good ole Highway 17 didn't cut through town anymore, but it came close enough. Many visitors stopped to see what was on the dealership lot before continuing to the car show in Monterey. Returning home, they'd tell stories of the cars at Ferrari of Los Gatos, helping the dealer become known worldwide.

As news of the dealership spread by word of mouth, it wasn't long before well-known movie stars, professional athletes, and other celebrities became regular customers. And some of the most successful Silicon Valley entrepreneurs made it a point to visit the dealer on the day their companies were acquired or went public. After all, it was Silicon Valley, and when reporters asked the overnight-millionaire CEOs what they were going to do with all the money, they often received this answer: "I'm going to buy a Ferrari." They'd worked hard to make their business succeed, and now they could afford to make another dream come true. Other executives loved stopping by to check out the classic cars and occasionally buy that unique model they just couldn't resist.

THE CEO WITHOUT A CHECKBOOK

It wasn't unusual to see famous people in the showroom right along with regular folks, and it was rare that anyone seemed out of place. However, one day, a well-known computer company CEO came by to look, and he was entirely unprepared.

"I went down there [Ferrari of Los Gatos] on a Sunday in shorts and a T-shirt," said James Treybig, the chief executive of Tandem Computer. His company had gone public in 1977, and while jogging through downtown Los Gatos, the 45-year-old CEO saw his dream car through the showroom window, a 1978 Ferrari 308 GTS. He wanted to buy the car but didn't have his checkbook. "They let me drive it off, and there was no way you could look at me and know I could pay for it."

That wasn't unusual for Brian. He was once quoted in the *New York Times* saying, "We're not so prim and proper that we won't let a guy take his car home just because he forgot his checkbook." That type of trusting attitude meant a lot to Treybig. "I'd worked hard, and you try to think of something that you dreamed of that makes it all worth it."

In 1984, venture capitalists funded computer start-ups like Tandem and referred to Santa Clara Valley (the area around Los Gatos) as the "major womb" of technology. William Draper III of Sutter Hill Ventures, one of the top venture capital firms in the United States, said, "The valley will remain this way because of Stanford [University], the original cell from which the whole body grew. All the parts are here. Circuit board stuffers, trade secret lawyers, and venture capitalists. There's even the Los Gatos Ferrari dealer."

Draper was right, and more than 35 years later, Silicon Valley remains a top spot for technology manufacturing companies, now minus the Los Gatos Ferrari dealer.

THE PROFESSOR AND HIS LAMBORGHINI

Stanford University is located 20 minutes north of Los Gatos and is known for educating some of the world's most brilliant people. Its faculty and alumni have founded many prominent technology companies, including Cisco, Google, Hewlett-Packard, LinkedIn, Silicon Graphics,

Sun Microsystems, and Yahoo!. Some alumni may not start well-known technology companies, but they can still make the headlines.

A professor from Stanford who wanted an exotic sports car did just that.

Simon walked into Ferrari of Los Gatos and exclaimed, "I'm writing a book and owe myself an exotic car." Intrigued, the salesman on the floor listened as Simon continued, "I have terrible credit, but I'm getting an advance on the book that will allow me to make a down payment."

Simon's eyes raced around the room at the cars on display.

"I want something different. I love Lamborghinis. Do you have any of those?"

Well, it so happened there was a Lamborghini Miura, a high-performance mid-engined sports car, sitting in the back section of the showroom. When his eyes met it, Simon fell in love.

"I want it! You must hold it for me until the end of the week."

Such requests were not uncommon, and the salesperson was happy to oblige. "Sure, we'll have the car and paperwork ready for you when you come back Friday."

Friday rolled around with no Simon. No-shows were not that uncommon at the dealership. Most customers who did not put a deposit down on a car didn't return or call if they changed their mind.

But this is not a story about an ordinary person.

Simon showed up the following day. "I'm here for my Lamborghini!" he shouted as he walked into the dealership.

He'd received the advance on his book and wanted to use it as a down payment. When he found out he could get a lease for the balance, Simon could hardly control his excitement.

Well, at least for the time being.

A few days went by, and Simon drove in, reporting something wrong with the car. The service technician found that the slave clutch mechanism needed replacement. Since Simon had just purchased the vehicle, the dealership agreed to replace the clutch mechanism at no charge and loaned him a green Ferrari 308 GT4 until the new part arrived.

As luck would have it, they could locate the part only at the Lamborghini factory in Sant'Agata Bolognese, a tiny Italian town. After a week,

Simon called to see if they had completed the work on his car. He appreciated the green Ferrari, but it didn't drive like his Lamborghini. The service department explained they were trying to get the part expressed by air from Europe but were at the mercy of the Lamborghini factory in Italy. However, they would let him know as soon as the part arrived.

Several more days went by, and Simon became impatient. When the days turned into weeks, his patience gave out. He drove to the dealership and returned the Ferrari loaner. Agitated, he seemed to be on the verge of a nervous breakdown. He screamed at the service department, "I want my Lamborghini back, and I want it to operate properly. I can't go on like this any longer." The service manager assured him they were doing everything they could and would call the factory in Italy again tomorrow.

The call to Italy wasn't necessary.

As the sun rose on Ferrari of Los Gatos the next day, a TV news crew set up near the Lamborghini in the service parking lot across the street. Minutes before the dealership opened, a second news crew arrived and shortly after that a third. Multiple news crews were unusual for East Main Street. Next, a group of motorcycle bikers showed up, circling the car, and a crowd started to gather. Finally, Simon arrived in a vehicle driven by a friend, right on cue. As he stepped out of the car with a sledgehammer in his hands, the news cameras began to roll. Without saying a word, Simon started beating his car with the sledgehammer. With a few swings, the headlights exploded, the hood caved in, and the windshield turned into a thousand pieces of glass. He invited the bikers to join him and finish the job.

The crowd gasped, and the camera crews, in shock and disbelief, filmed the spectacle from every angle. No one had ever seen anything like this before.

By the time police officers arrived, the car looked like it had been in a terrible accident. The police talked to Simon for a few minutes, and then he got into his friend's car, and they drove away. The police dispersed the crowd and walked across the street to the dealership.

"Why didn't you arrest this guy and put him in jail?" Brian asked.

"Well, it is his car, after all," the officer in charge answered. "Since his car was on your lot, which is private property, he can do whatever he wants with it—as long as he doesn't break any laws. If he decides he wants to beat the crap out of his car, there is nothing we can do about it."

Next, the television news crews walked across the street to get the rest of the story.

"I don't know what to tell you," Brian began. "We sold Simon a car, and he had to bring it back for a clutch problem that required that we replace a part. We had to order that part from the Lamborghini factory in Italy, and since we knew it would take some time to get it, we loaned him a Ferrari to drive until the part came in. It has taken longer than anyone expected, and the part has still not arrived from Italy. Yesterday, he returned our Ferrari loaner and today destroyed his car." Brian shook his head as he looked at the wreckage that was once a special edition Lamborghini. "Even so, I just don't understand why someone would do this to such a beautiful car."

Simon's crazy antics earned him airtime on Silicon Valley television stations and several syndicated news channels across the nation. The evening news commentators opened with, "In a small town in Silicon Valley California, Los Gatos, or 'The Cats,' home to Ferrari of Los Gatos, a customer of the exclusive car dealership decided to . . ." The newscast continued with Simon acting like a maniac, destroying a beautiful, expensive, exotic Italian sports car on Main Street. Now, everyone in the San Francisco Bay Area and the rest of the country knew about the Los Gatos Ferrari dealership and its holdings of hard-to-find cars. Sometimes unexpected events that don't make sense at the time turn out to be just what you needed. This newsworthy spectacle was brilliant—and the nationwide marketing didn't cost Ferrari of Los Gatos a cent. Business at the dealership picked up the very next day, and customers started coming in droves.

But the story doesn't end here.

Simon never contacted Ferrari of Los Gatos again and never claimed the car's leftovers. A few months had gone by, and Brian didn't think about it anymore. One day, though, he received a phone call from one of his employees.

"Turn on your TV. You won't believe who's on the news."

The same television stations that had covered the Lamborghini beating were now reporting the arrest of a suspected bank robber in San Rafael, a city about two hours north of Los Gatos. As police led the alleged thief to jail, the wind flipped his hoody back and exposed his face. It was Simon. News cameras were filming him again, but he would not be allowed to walk away from his escapades this time.

Simon turned out to be an ex-felon who'd spent most of his adult life in San Quentin, a prison near San Rafael where Johnny Cash had performed a concert to the inmates' cheers and applause. On his release, Simon had stolen a college professor's name and identity to purchase the Lamborghini from Ferrari of Los Gatos. No wonder he never came back.

An article in the *California Today* newspaper by Susan Hathaway on June 24, 1979, discussing businesses in Los Gatos, commented about Brian's fabled customer. "Longtime town residents still can't get used to some of the strange behavior of Burnett's moneyed clients. Like the fellow who thought his Lamborghini had been in the shop too long, so he marched down to the dealership with two burly bodyguards and demolished the car with a crowbar before the shocked mechanics and onlookers."

And what happened to the car?

An insurance company bought the wrecked Lamborghini Miura and resold it to someone who wanted to put it back into running condition. When that turned out to be too costly, the car became a source of hard-to-find parts.

Ironic, because that's what got it destroyed in the first place.

BREEZIN' WITH MR. OCTOBER IN A RED CADILLAC

The Mountain Winery in Saratoga attracted thousands of people to sold-out concerts, and George Benson was one of the favorite performers. His 1976 hit song "Breezin'" made him a jazz-pop guitar superstar. George made it a point to visit Ferrari of Los Gatos as part of us annual routine. He didn't always buy a car, but he couldn't perform at the winery without first looking at the cars on the dealership lot.

One year, a 1959 red Cadillac convertible caught his eye.

Sales manager Dennis Glavis recalled that visit.

"I enjoyed seeing him each year. He was such a nice guy and always a real gentleman. The time he came in and spotted that convertible Cadillac, it was love at first sight."

George spent a long time checking the car out. After glancing under the car, he looked up at Dennis and said, "I just might buy this car." When it got to be midday, he couldn't make up his mind. He decided to go have lunch, thinking that might clear his mind.

When he turned to leave, the showroom door opened, and George was staring into the eyes of Mr. October.

In Major League Baseball, October is the month of postseason playoff games and World Series heroics. Reggie Jackson was nicknamed "Mr. October" for his clutch hitting in the postseason with the Oakland Athletics and New York Yankees. In game 6 of the 1977 World Series between the Yankees and Dodgers, Reggie hit three home runs, all on the first pitch thrown to him by three different Dodger pitchers. That feat tied a record set by Babe Ruth. And since Reggie had hit a home run in his last at bat in game 5, his three home runs in game 6 equaled four home runs on four consecutive swings against four Dodgers pitchers. He became the first player to win the World Series Most Valuable Player award for two different teams.

After the game, Yankee catcher Thurmon Munson walked up to his teammate and said, "Nice job, Mr. October." Reggie replied, "Mr. October? I think I'll keep that name." And the baseball world has known Reggie Jackson, number 44, as Mr. October ever since.

It turned out that George and Reggie shared a passion for classic cars and enjoyed hanging out around Ferrari of Los Gatos. They had a lot to talk about, and George wasn't about to leave now.

"Reggie, look at this convertible Cadillac. What do you think about it?" Reggie loved it too.

After giving that car the once-over, they decided to walk across the street. They returned shortly with one of their favorite beverages and decided to sit in the convertible with the top down on the showroom floor. They enjoyed each other's company and delighted the staff by hanging around.

George decided the Cadillac would be taking him to the Mountain Winery that evening. Then he'd have it shipped to his home after the performance. It is uncertain what influence Reggie had on the decision, but having his new friend agree it was a cool car probably made the decision a little easier, especially when your friend is Mr. October.

HE WANTED TO SHOW THE FERRARI TO HIS WIFE

On a warm, breezy afternoon, a gentleman dressed in a suit and tie walked into the dealership inquiring about a new maroon-colored Ferrari 308 GTSi on display.

"I drove by and noticed the car through the showroom window. I think this might be just the right color I was looking for."

Jack Gordon, one of the top salesmen at Ferrari of Los Gatos, pointed out the car's features and had the customer sit in the driver's seat. Luckily for Jack, the man didn't ask many questions and just wanted to know what it would cost. Jack's first offer was at the manufacturer's suggested retail price (MSRP), the right place to start negotiating. To Jack's surprise, the gentleman responded, "I think we can work that out. Could I bring my wife to look at the car tomorrow and go for a ride in it?"

"Sure, no problem. See you tomorrow."

Jack wasn't sure the man would come back, but if he did, he'd be ready to convince his wife the Ferrari was a great deal.

The gentleman returned the next day.

"Where's your wife?" asked Jack.

"She's at home. Can we stop by and show the car to her? We live in the condominiums over on Lark Avenue, a few miles from here. Can we do that?"

Jack nodded and said, "Let me get the keys."

Jack carefully pulled the Ferrari out of the showroom, parked, and waited for the customer to get into the car. As they buckled their seat belts, he roared the engine a few times to demonstrate the car's power. They were all smiles as they took off, with Jack accelerating as he shifted through the gears.

When they reached Lark Avenue, the customer motioned for Jack to park on the side street by the condominium complex. He got out of the car and said, "This Ferrari's great. Wait here, and I'll go get my wife."

A few minutes later, he returned and apologized for his wife taking so long.

"She wanted to change before going for a ride. I'll go get her and be right back."

Jack got out of the car to stretch his legs. Relaxing on the sidewalk, he noticed a man walking toward him. Jack started to say hello, but before he could, the stranger pushed a newspaper into his side, exposing a gun hidden underneath.

"Okay, now, don't give us any trouble. We don't want to hurt you," said the gunman.

You've got to be kidding me, Jack thought. *I'm getting robbed while I'm waiting for a customer.*

Jack hadn't made the connection—yet. There was no wife, there was no customer, and the men were working together. They weren't robbing him; they were stealing the Ferrari.

The gunman walked Jack to an isolated area in a park nearby. Jack had visions of being shot and left to die in the park. His heart was beating so fast he thought it would pop out of his chest.

"Take off your pants and stand up next to that tree," the gunman said. Then he handcuffed him to the tree.

"Don't make a sound for 20 minutes, and nothing will happen to you. Someone will be watching you, and if you don't follow my instructions, he'll shoot you."

A few minutes later, Jack could hear the roar of the Ferrari's engine drifting off in the distance.

When he couldn't hear the car anymore, he tried to get out of the handcuffs. They were tight. He struggled and struggled, pulling as hard as he could. Suddenly, to his surprise, the tree came out of the ground, roots and all. The tree was partially dead, and the hollow trunk had weak roots. But the handcuffs were too tight to get off the tree. He was free to walk, but the tree was coming with him.

Jack and the tree walked down Lark Avenue. He stopped at the first apartment building he came to and knocked on the nearest door. When two girls answered, they saw Jack, with no pants, handcuffed to a tree. They closed the door quickly and said they'd call the police.

It didn't take long for the police to arrive, free Jack of the handcuffs and his tree, and give him a ride back to Ferrari of Los Gatos. He explained what happened, but the police could not find the car or Jack's pants. The car thieves knew what they were doing. They had vanished along with the Ferrari.

Over time, Jack and the other sales staff stopped talking about the tale of the stolen Ferrari—until four years later, when Ferrari of Los Gatos received a phone call from Bakersfield, California.

"Do you guys own a Ferrari with dealer license plates?" the manager of a storage facility asked. After a quick vehicle identification number (VIN) check, Brian realized that they had stumbled on the car stolen from Jack.

The caller explained that some guy had come in regularly and paid cash for the storage unit. When he didn't show up for several months, as is the usual procedure, they cut the lock off and found nothing inside except the Ferrari.

When Brian asked how they knew to call Ferrari of Los Gatos, the manager answered, "Your name and phone number are on the sticker glued to the window on the car."

After four lost years, the brand-new car returned to Ferrari of Los Gatos.

The car needed dust removal, new fluids, and wax before it occupied the same spot on the showroom floor it had four years earlier. And not long after that, some lucky customer bought a four-year-old Ferrari 308 GTSi with only 300 miles on the odometer.

JACK AND THE CAR HE COULDN'T DRIVE

In 1975, the San Francisco Giants drafted Jack Clark at the age of 19. He became one of the most feared hitters in the National League throughout his Major League Baseball career. Jack received the Silver Slugger Award twice as the best offensive first baseman in the National League. And his

26-game hitting streak in 1978 is still the longest by any Giants player since 1900.

After baseball, Jack's favorite pastime was owning cars and drag racing. In 1989, he purchased his first Ferrari, a Mondial t, mid-engined, V-8–powered luxury touring car, from Ferrari of Los Gatos. Conceived as a "practical" Ferrari, the Mondial t was a genuine long-distance four-seater with sufficient headroom and legroom in the backseat for children or a small adult.

Jack and his family arrived at Ferrari of Los Gatos to pick up the Mondial t—a $75,000 ($160,000 in 2021 dollars) car they laid eyes on for the first time.

After finishing the paperwork and paying for the car, Jack put the kids in the backseat and slid in behind the steering wheel. After a couple of minutes, Brian looked out the window and told his salesman, "Your customer isn't moving."

The salesman thought maybe the emergency brake won't go off and walked out to help. He returned to Brian with a smile on his face. "I've got to teach him how to drive a stick shift." So Jack Clark, one of the most talented hitters in baseball, struck out driving his new car—he hadn't realized this Ferrari came with only a manual transmission.

For the next hour or so, Jack received "how-to-drive-a-stick-shift lessons" at the Los Gatos High School parking lot.

Jack enjoyed driving his Ferrari Mondial t and returned a year later to purchase a 1990 Ferrari F40. A successful ballplayer by all measures, Jack wasn't so successful with his fast cars. In 1992, he was driven into bankruptcy, caused partially by his insatiable appetite for luxury cars. At the time, his collection included 18 vehicles ranging from GM vans to Mercedes and Fords as well as two Ferraris and a Rolls-Royce. The cars, worth more than $1.7 million ($3.2 million in 2021 dollars), spanned 60 years from the 1930s to the 1990s.

Two of these cars exceeded the value of all the others together—the Ferraris.

KIDNAPPED IN BEVERLY HILLS

Rueben not only picked up cars for Ferrari of Los Gatos but delivered them as well. One delivery was a black Ferrari Mondial Cabriolet headed for Hollywood. It wasn't unusual for celebrities to purchase a car sight unseen, and that's what entertainer and movie star Cher had done.

Brian had told Rueben to leave Los Gatos early, deliver the car to Beverly Hills, and take a flight back to the San Jose airport. Rueben left on time for the six-hour drive. At about 4 p.m., Brian received a phone call from the salesman who'd gone to the airport to pick up Rueben.

"He wasn't on the flight."

Concerned, Brian called Rueben, who answered, alive and well, and said, "She won't let me leave."

"Rueben, what are you talking about."

"Hello?" a female voice came on.

"Who's this?"

"This is Cher, and you leave Rueben alone. We're having fun together, and he'll be back when he gets back. Understood?"

"Well, I . . . hello?"

Cher had hung up, and Brian decided there's nothing he could or should do. He'd wait until Rueben called for someone to pick him up at the airport or just see him when he got back.

Rueben came to work the next day and had to field many questions from the Ferrari of Los Gatos staff.

"Well, she held me there for a long time. She's a great person. She showed me every room in her house. It's huge. Every time I said I needed to go, she said, 'Have another drink.'"

He did have a gift from Cher for everyone. She had asked him the name of every person who worked at Ferrari of Los Gatos. In an envelope she sent with Rueben was a personalized autographed photo for each of his coworkers.

About a year later, Rueben saw a picture of the Ferrari he'd delivered to Cher in the newspaper. Her boyfriend had smashed it up a little. The newspaper headline read, "Cher, friend say media to blame for the incident." It seems her boyfriend lost control of the Ferrari and struck a photographer's car as he entered the driveway of Cher's home. By accident, of course.

THE REDHEAD THAT ARRIVED LATE

In September 1989, Beverly Hills exotic car dealer Rick Black contacted Ferrari dealers across the United States looking for the best deal on a 1990 red-on-tan Ferrari Testarossa, Testarossa being the Italian word for "redhead." This model was the hottest-selling Ferrari on the planet. Demand was so high that they were selling at a steep premium over the MSRP. It turned out that Ferrari of Los Gatos had the best combination of price ($300,000) and delivery (March 1990). Rick Black instructed his attorney to negotiate a contract to purchase the car. The attorney wrote a letter requesting an agreement between Ferrari of Los Gatos and Black on Black, Rick Black's company. A check for a $50,000 down payment accompanied the letter.

As time went by, Testarossa demand kept increasing, and it seemed the price went up daily. When Testarossas arrived from the factory, they were worth more than when they were sold, meaning that Ferrari of Los Gatos left money on the table with every car it sold. However, even though the dealership had sold them below the current market value, it was still making a high profit (sometimes as high as 60 percent), and the cars weren't sitting on the showroom floor.

A few months passed, and Testarossa supply was finally outpacing demand. As a result, it was difficult to sell one at the MSRP.

When Mr. Black learned of this pricing shift, he called Ferrari of Los Gatos, requesting to cancel the contract and asking for his money back.

"What are you talking about?" asked Brian.

"Well, prices are coming down, and I'm going to lose money on this deal."

"You are a car dealer yourself, so I know you know how this works. Sometimes you make money, sometimes you lose."

Mr. Black didn't care about that truism. Instead, he wanted his $50,000 deposit back.

In reality, it wasn't a deposit at all; it was a down payment on a signed contract that stated that "when the car arrives, Black on Black owes Ferrari of Los Gatos $250,000."

"Now, Mr. Black, when that car was going up in value, would you have let me return your $50,000 so I could sell it to someone else for more money?"

"Of course not!"

"Then, what is it that you don't understand? If you don't want the car, we'll sell it to someone else for as much as it will bring, and you'll owe the deficit up to the original selling price of $300,000."

The conversation didn't last long after that, and Mr. Black never called Brian again.

However, several months later, a tower of a man looking like a football player arrived at Ferrari of Los Gatos. He walked through the lot into the showroom and demanded to speak with Mr. Burnett in private.

When they sat down in Brian's office, he raised his head, straightened his back, and displayed the muscles in his 300-pound frame.

"Mr. Black sent me here to pick up a check for $50,000."

"What's your name?" Brian asked.

"My friends call me Big Mike."

"Now, why would he want a check for $50,000 from us, Mike?"

"Well, he gave you $50,000 as a deposit on a car he's decided against and would like his money back."

Brian leaned forward, paused, and tried to clarify things.

"Number one, that money was not a deposit, Mike. It was a down payment on a purchase contract. So, number two naturally follows, meaning he ain't getting his money back."

Mike started to respond, and Brian interrupted him. "Let me make this very clear, that money's gone. The contract he and I signed tied up the car, and I couldn't sell it to anyone else. If your boss had wanted the car when it came in, he could have paid the balance, taken it, and sold it. But, since your boss didn't do that, we sold the car at a lower wholesale price, so the 50 is gone. Now, he wouldn't want his down payment back if the value of the car had gone up, would he?"

Big Mike looked Brian over and leaned in with his chest extended, arms out and hands open.

"I can understand your point, Mr. Burnett, but I have a job to do, and I need to leave here with $50,000."

Brian's friend Steve, the retired police officer who accompanied Brian on deliveries and hung out at Ferrari of Los Gatos, overheard the conversation from the hallway. As a cop, he had been in challenging situations and seen things you couldn't and probably wouldn't want to imagine. A well-spoken, polite, and intelligent person, Steve knew how to become a badass if necessary.

Steve walked into the office, the gun he carried visible, and said, "I don't like your tone of voice with Mr. Burnett, and I think you better get back in your car right now. And, let me tell you something else. If I ever see you here again, you won't be leavin' in a car."

Mike stood up slowly, turned toward the door, and left the office, his eyes glued to the floor. He walked out to his car and drove off. Ferrari of Los Gatos never heard from Big Mike again. Steve had a way of persuading people.

But Black on Black didn't stop there. In the summer of 1992, Black on Black filed a petition with the State of California New Motor Vehicle Board attempting to recover its $50,000 down payment. After a year of legal negotiations, the board proposed a settlement and ordered Ferrari of Los Gatos to pay $15,000 to Black on Black, and the case was closed.

I'M UNTOUCHABLE

Big Rudy was known as the largest cocaine supplier in California history. He grew up in North Oakland's Bushrod neighborhood, where he played basketball, football, and baseball at the nearby recreation center and park. He did well lifting weights and started showing promise on the bodybuilding scene, winning several local competitions, but cars were his first love. He started the Camaro club with some of his childhood friends. What started out as a group buying and fixing up '68 Chevy Camaros, eventually turned into an auto theft ring. That's what first got Rudy in trouble with the law. He was arrested and sent to federal prison for three years. Those years would turn out to be life changing.

In prison, he became good friends with a Colombian drug trafficker from the Medellín Cartel. They spent a lot of time working out together, and Rudy made sure nobody messed around with the Colombian. Not only did they become workout buddies and best friends, but they also started planning their takeover of the Oakland drug trade. With the unlimited supply of cocaine from the Colombian connection, Rudy was able to control the local drug trade.

In 1987, he appeared on television telling a news reporter, "I'm untouchable! I'll never get arrested."

A few weeks later, federal agents proved him wrong.

Living in a 6,400-square-foot mansion in the Napa Valley wine country called "sky castle," his home had more security than a military fortress. But after boasting on television, an army of agents raided Rudy's home and confiscated 90 pounds of cocaine.

While Rudy publicly said there was no way he'd ever go to jail, he'd been preparing for the inevitable in private.

Several days earlier, Brian had received a phone call from his friend Roy saying he knew a guy who had some cars to sell. He went on to say this guy was a friend of "Big" Rudy Henderson. Rudy was afraid that if he did get arrested, the feds would confiscate his collection of classic cars.

Roy explained that it had to be a cash transaction and that it had to happen quickly. "If you don't come up here tonight, you probably won't get a shot at 'em."

Brian spent the rest of the day getting his hands on as much cash as he could. He had a few friends who would provide some money to him when he needed to buy cars—for a slice of the deal, of course. Later that night, he met Roy and Rudy's friend Eddie.

Roy introduced the two, and the first thing Eddie said was, "This is a cash deal, Brian, and it has to go down pretty much immediately." Brian nodded, Roy got into the backseat, and Eddie rode shotgun in Brian's BMW M6. Their first stop was a warehouse in Benicia. They arrived at midnight. They didn't want anybody like the feds to see what was going on. Brian was nervous carrying so much cash around, but there was no one else at the warehouse, Roy was a good friend, and Eddie seemed trustworthy.

There were about 10 cars at the warehouse. Brian wrote down the makes and models, which included Corvettes, Rolls-Royces, Mercedes, and Bentleys, and agreed to buy them all. "I can let you know what they're worth first thing in the morning."

"We're not done yet. Let's take a ride."

They drove back over the bridge into Oakland, and Brian got a little more anxious as the night went on. "I didn't realize this was going to take so long. We stopped at a bar, and Eddie told us to wait in the car. After a few minutes, he came out and motioned us out of the vehicle. We walked to a building behind the bar that had another five or six of Rudy's cars in it. When we came to an agreement that I'd buy those, I jumped back in the car as fast as I could. Next, we headed to Rudy's mother's house. In her backyard were three more cars. I said okay to those as well, praying this was the end."

Not so lucky. There were still a couple more houses to go.

Well into the night, Eddie turned to Brian. "Okay, that's all of them."

Brian dropped off Roy and Eddie, then drove home. It had been a long night, and he didn't get home until 5 a.m. "I didn't get much sleep, but I made a deal on the cars, and while none of them were killer studs, they were all sellable. So I arranged for them to be picked up the next day after making sure the title papers were in order and paying Eddie the cash. None of the cars were in Rudy's name. They were in his mom's name, his brother's name, his uncle's name, you know, whoever. I paid $230,000 cash for all of them."

Two days later, federal agents raided Rudy's Napa Valley mansion and charged him with several drug trafficking and manufacturing charges. Immediately, the feds went to confiscate the cars and discovered they were gone. It didn't take them long to figure out where they went.

About a week later, five federal agents walked into Ferrari of Los Gatos and asked to speak with Brian Burnett.

"I'm Brian Burnett. What can I do for you?"

"We'd like to speak with you in private."

Brian escorted them into his office and brought in more chairs. All the agents sat down and looked at Brian, but only one spoke. "We notice you have some cars on your lot that interest us. We believe they belong to a person named Rudy Henderson."

"Well, I found out they were available, and I bought them all. But not from Mr. Henderson. None of them were in his name, gentlemen."

"Did you know him at the time?"

"I knew of him, but I'd never met him personally."

"Can we look at the paperwork?"

"Yup," Brian said, feigning confidence, but he couldn't help but think, *I'm in trouble, and I'm going to lose the $230,000.*

He handed the title papers to them, and they proceeded out to the lot and walked around to match the cars to the titles.

When they returned to the office, the only agent who spoke said, "Can we talk?"

Brian remembered the sick feeling in his stomach walking back to his office with the agents. "I was so worried that I was shaking. I didn't know if I'd done something illegal or what. And I worried that maybe I'd been screwed by Rudy."

Back in Brian's office, they handed him the title paperwork.

"You won this one."

"What do you mean?"

"We were getting ready to confiscate these cars." The agent squinted at Brian. "You beat us to the punch. Good luck with 'em 'cause there's nothing we can do. You bought 'em fair and square, you got the titles, and we can't take 'em away from you." The agent nodded to his associates signaling that it was time to leave.

After the agents left, Brian collapsed into his chair.

He breathed a sigh of relief and figured he'd never see the feds again. Wrong.

About a year later, agents returned to Ferrari of Los Gatos, accusing Brian of money laundering. It seems another car dealer, angry with Brian, told the FBI he was laundering money through his muscle car business, Nostalgia Motors. Brian remembered the day that two federal agents came into the dealership. "The FBI agents asked to speak with me and said, 'You are under investigation, and should hire an attorney.' They told me that another car dealer turned me in. Evidently, they couldn't figure out how I'd had gotten my hands on that much cash." It wasn't unusual for Brian to stroll into the bank with $75,000 cash included in his daily deposit. He had wealthy clients who sometimes paid in cash. At the time, banking laws did not require a customer to disclose the source of large cash deposits.

The feds asked Brian questions that he answered and then made comments such as, "You sure got a nice big house up on the hill, Mr. Burnett," to which Brian would simply respond, "That nice big house has a nice big mortgage on it." Even so, no one really believed that Ferrari of Los Gatos could make enough money legally for Brian to build a 5,000-square-foot home in the hills above Los Gatos. Brian realized he needed an attorney. He interviewed two young men and an older gentleman. He hired the older gentleman, who reminded him of his grandfather. "That attorney didn't seem to have a care in the world and acted like he could handle anything that came his way. That's probably why he reminded me of my grandfather. I gave him a box containing Nostalgia Motors car sales records and he told me to go home, relax, and that he'd take care of everything."

A couple months went by when Brian received a call from the attorney's assistant saying he could come and pick up his documents, the case was closed. When Brian arrived at the attorney's office, he asked, "How did you do this? You never called me once to ask any questions."

The attorney responded, "Well, I've been at this a long time Mr. Burnett. I worked for the government most of my life. I was an IRS agent stationed at Pearl Harbor in 1941. I watched the December 7 attack from my office window."

"That's incredible."

"I know how to talk to federal employees such as IRS and FBI agents. I explained to them what's really going on here, and they decided not to pursue you. So, the case is closed."

Once again, Brian thought the feds were gone, but he'd be wrong.

In 1989, two years after his arrest, Rudy pleaded guilty to possession for sale of 7 kilograms (15.4 pounds) of cocaine and tax evasion totaling $115,000. He also agreed to forfeit his Sonoma County estate and the only two cars he had left. He received a 20-year prison sentence.

Rudy was paroled from federal prison early and, in 2002, started Rudy's Beautys, a used car dealership in Oakland. In December 2006, as he sat in a car outside a famous soul food restaurant, Lois the Pie Queen, a man approached the vehicle and shot him multiple times, killing him instantly. Rudy was 57 years old.

Drug dealers played their part in the history of Ferrari of Los Gatos. They weren't dealing drugs; they just seemed to love hanging around the dealership and the cars. The fact they could buy one of those cars with no questions asked appealed to them. Brian didn't discriminate whom he sold to. It didn't matter if you were a drug dealer, a celebrity, or just a regular guy who loved Ferraris. Customers were happy that the dealership would move heaven and earth to locate the car to satisfy that hard-to-find request.

And customers believed that if Ferrari of Los Gatos couldn't find the car you wanted, no one could.

Chapter Twelve

The Stone

(1992)

DURING THE 1960S, CHUCK HILL WAS ONE OF THE MOST TALENTED CAR individuals in Santa Clara Valley. He helped run Bob Sykes Dodge, the same dealership Brian had managed years earlier, and he knew everyone at the other dealerships on Stevens Creek Boulevard. At the time, more cars were sold on that boulevard (referred to as "the Creek" by car dealers) than any other street in California, maybe in the nation. People who knew Chuck either loved him or hated him, but everyone agreed he knew the car business better than anyone else around. After retirement, he hung out at Ferrari of Los Gatos. He loved being around the place.

Brian respected Chuck as one of the most talented car guys he knew. "Chuck was the type of guy that if you had 20 grand in your pocket, he'd figure a way to take it. But if you were his friend, needed 20 grand, and he had it, he'd give it to you."

One day, he came into Brian's office and sat down.

"You've got the stone."

"What?"

"You've got to be very careful; you've got the stone."

Brian knew Chuck was a little unusual and liked to smoke grass and drink tequila and figured that he was either high or having one of his crazy fits.

"I don't understand what you are talking about Chuck."

"You've got the stone, and everybody's after it. I've been on the Creek, and everybody wants your stone."

It still didn't make sense to Brian.

"You've got the stone. Haven't you seen the movie?"

"What movie?"

"*Romancing the Stone* with Michael Douglas and Danny DeVito. Everyone in the movie is after the treasure map to find El Corazón, the emerald stone. Ferrari of Los Gatos is that stone."

Brian should have paid more attention to Chuck instead of thinking he'd had too much tequila. After all, the boys at North Bay Ford were raising flooring costs every chance they got, others were trying to convince Brian to let them take over the business, and Ferrari was showing signs of wanting the dealership as well. Everyone had an angle.

It might be another one of those coincidences, but Robert Zemeckis, the director of *Romancing the Stone*, also directed the 1980s movie *Used Cars*, which told the story of two brothers who were rival car dealers. When one brother finds out a proposed freeway exit will demolish his dealership, he starts scheming to find a way to take over his brother's dealership across the street. Taking over dealerships and stealing someone's jewel seemed to be the thing in the 1980s, and Ferrari of Los Gatos was no exception.

Brian knew that he had a good thing and that his business was probably the most lucrative and visible car dealership in California, maybe even throughout the country. Ferrari of Los Gatos was well known everywhere, but Brian never thought of it as that big of a deal. He was living his dream, doing well, and enjoying every minute of it, but to him, it was just selling cars. He was proud that even at the height of his success, he never changed the way he treated people or cared about them.

The business had always been decent, but sometimes, special events caused spikes in sales. For example, the introduction of the 1976 308 GTB was an answer to Ferrari enthusiasts' prayers. The 1974 308 GT4 2+2 with its Bertone box-like design had never really caught on, and some called it ugly. So Ferrari returned to Pininfarina for the 308 GTB's styling, and the two-seat, mid-engined coupe, eight inches shorter than the GT4, turned out to be a hit.

Then, in 1980, Ferrari made a mistake, and sales tanked. The 308 GTBi and GTSi models were plagued by an oil consumption issue when Bosch K-Jetronic mechanical fuel injectors replaced carburetors. But

Enzo did the right thing, announcing he would replace the motors in any car that had a problem. It was a difficult time, but dealers got through it. When car sales halted, Ferrari paid the dealers to replace engines, offsetting some of their losses. Again, Enzo treated the dealers fairly.

In 1982, when Ferrari introduced the 308 Quattrovalvole with four-valve heads, in GTB and GTS form, Ferrari sales started a steady climb that continued every year afterward. People were now on waiting lists to buy. And in 1988, the year Enzo died, the Ferrari market went absurd. Brian likened it to a runaway stock market. "With the artist dead, Ferraris started going up faster than anyone expected. I mean, someone would call us on a car, and in five minutes, we had it sold with a $35,000 profit, all on a phone call. And we never touched most of the cars. We'd buy them with a phone call, sell them with a phone call, and set up delivery with a phone call."

Brian and New York Ferrari dealer Steven Kessler helped establish the market for these cars. They spoke almost daily about what price models should bring. Some might call it simple trial and error, but there was a method to their madness. Their motto became, "Forget the listed price. This is the selling price." If they stuck to their guns and someone bought the car, it became the new market value. If a car was struggling to sell at a price, they lowered it a little to see what would happen. Even if it took a little longer to sell, the car eventually went close to that price. The next time one of those models came on the market, everyone knew what the market price should be ahead of time. And this helped other dealers as well. When a customer came in thinking their car was worth a certain amount, the dealer could point to ads on either coast of the country and ask, "If Ferrari of Los Gatos has your car listed at this price, how can your car be worth more?"

Brian and Steven were setting the market when nobody else would. It worked on Ferraris, so they used the same approach with other classic cars as well. "Steve and I believed that every car had its true value, and we were happy to help our friends at the other dealerships find it."

Brian defined those times. "I had Camelot. Nothing went wrong, every day got better, and everyone was happy."

It wasn't unusual for Ferrari of Los Gatos to make $100,000 in a day. And there was a time when customers would offer double the sticker price on a new Ferrari to avoid the waiting list. "If a car normally sold for $100,000, they begged us to take $200,000. And, we had to think about it. It was just nuts."

In 1989, things changed.

When an artist dies, the value of their work can soar higher than they ever imagined. Vincent Van Gogh struggled financially during his life-time. He only sold one painting while he was alive, *Red Vineyard at Arles*, in 1890 and received 400 Belgian francs ($78 then, $1,000 in 2021). In 1990, his painting *The Portrait of Doctor Gachet* sold at auction for $82.5 million in three minutes.

Like a famous artist, the 1988 death of Enzo Ferrari dramatically increased the value of the cars displaying his name. Car values did not change when Henry Ford, Walter Chrysler, Louis Chevrolet, or even Maserati, Lamborghini, or Porsche died. But Enzo Ferrari had created the most valuable automobile marque in the world and, unlike other automobile manufacturers, retained control of Ferrari until his death. Even when he sold half the company to Fiat in 1969, he ensured the contracts gave him complete control while he was alive. After that, Fiat would have to decide how to run Ferrari.

At Ferrari of Los Gatos, news of Enzo's death brought sadness and concern, especially for Brian. He'd been mesmerized by Ferrari's cars since he was 12 years old. Living around the Ferrari cars he loved to sell, Brian developed respect and admiration for the man from Maranello. He realized how lucky he was to live and breathe his childhood dream day in and day out. He wondered what it would be like without Il Commendatore around anymore.

But his thoughts were redirected by the excitement of the F40.

Enzo had spoken a year before his death at a ceremony commemo-rating his company's 40th anniversary at Maranello's factory. Through an interpreter, he unveiled the Ferrari model F40.

"A little more than a year ago, I expressed my wish to the engineers. Build a car to be the best in the world. And now, the car is here."

Ferrari engineers had designed the F40 to be the fastest road vehicle ever built. They viewed the Porsche 959 as their primary competition. In the mid-1980s, Porsche shocked the world with its 959 supercars. With their flat-six engine and a total output of 450 horsepower, they soon became known as the "world's fastest car." That didn't sit well with Enzo, so he challenged his engineers to design a faster car. The Porsche designers equipped the 959S with luxury amenities, while the F40 was all nuts and bolts. Every spoiler on the F40 played a vital role in keeping the car on the ground at high speed, and every vent was essential to keep the brakes and engine cool.

The Porsche could get from 0 to 60 mph in 3.5 seconds and had a top speed of 198 mph. The F40 could get to 60 mph in under four seconds but had a top speed of 201 mph, making it 1988's "world's fastest car." Ferrari announced they would build 200 F40s for the North American market and did just that. Over the next two years, Ferrari produced 1,311 F40s, and 213 were shipped to North America.

Brian and his sales team contacted customers, letting them know the F40 was coming and would probably be the wildest thing ever built by Ferrari. The interest was unparalleled. Brian wondered what the car would bring given that Ferrari would make only a limited number. They said the car might sell for $50,000 over the list price, and no one batted an eye. They tried $100,000 over and had the same reaction—none. Every two or three days, they increased the price by another $100,000. Finding no resistance, Brian contacted everyone on the waiting list to let them know the price had changed to market, meaning that whenever an F40 arrived, it would sell at the current market price. If anyone did not want to pay the current market price, Brian would offer the car to the next person on the list.

The excitement was growing, and interest in the F40 was spreading like wildfire. Calls were coming in every day asking when it would arrive. Some callers weren't buyers; they just wanted to see the F40 when it arrived at Ferrari of Los Gatos.

The big day came.

Late one afternoon, the first F40 rolled out of a van onto Pageant Way. Brian got in and fired it up. As the car idled, the passenger door opened, and his son Greg jumped in. "Let's go, Dad." After school, Greg had stopped by the dealership, knowing that today was the day the new Ferrari would show up.

"We have to watch the gauges, Greg," Brian cautioned his son, "and make sure we warm up the car before we take it out." When the car was ready, they headed down Main Street. After all, Brian wasn't exactly sure how the F40 would respond when he pushed the gas pedal.

They headed past the Los Gatos Lodge and entered Highway 17, heading toward San Jose. Brian's foot gently pressed the gas pedal. He remembered that one of his sales staff had smashed a new Testarossa driving it for the first time and didn't want to repeat that. Pushing the gas pedal was mesmerizing, and soon, other cars on the highway became blurs.

"How fast are we going, Dad?"

Stunned when he glanced at the speedometer, Brian realized the needle was at 145 mph. The car had accelerated so smoothly he didn't realize how fast they were going.

Returning to the dealership, they sat in the car, staring straight ahead. Brian described the moment. "We got back to the dealership, and my mind was, Greg's mind was, our minds were completely blown."

The first customer on the waiting list was Bill, one of the founders of cable TV in the Northwest. Anything Bill bought went through Jack Gordon, the first salesperson Ferrari of Los Gatos had hired. "Give him a call, Jack. It's a million over."

The price, $1 million over whatever Ferrari put on the window sticker as the suggested retail price, had been Brian's decision. That made the first F40 go for around $1.4 million ($3.2 million in 2021 dollars).

The price Jack quoted when he called didn't shock Bill. Instead, he simply said, "Well, that's fine, Jack, but I have a few cars I'd like to use as trade-ins, if I could?"

Brian remembered the transaction because it involved five trade-ins, something very unusual in the car business.

"Now, think about this for a second. Bill trades in a 427 SC Cobra [worth $1.6 million in 2021], a Mercedes 300 SL Gullwing [worth $1.4 million in 2021], a '53 Cadillac El Dorado convertible [worth $250,000 in 2021], a couple of other cars I can't remember and gives us $300,000 cash. And the cars were in mint perfect condition."

The Gullwing Mercedes and the '53 Eldo were in a pristine condition. Classic cars like these were seldom seen at public auctions, but Brian took them both to the Kruse International auction. The Kruse family conducted the world's first consignment collector car auction in 1971 at Auburn, Indiana. The event was held annually after that each Labor Day weekend. It attracted 200,000 attendees and exhibited 5,000 collectible vehicles. Between 1985 and 1987, Kruse sold 1,000 cars from the Bill Harrah collection for a total of $41 million ($107 million in 2021 dollars). The success of these events led the Kruse family to help Tom Barrett start the annual Barrett-Jackson auction in Scottsdale, Arizona.

Just like his desire to sell Ferraris to the average man on the street, Brian enjoyed making hard-to-find classic cars available at both auction events as well.

Kruse and Barrett-Jackson are considered two of the world's greatest classic car auctions. Every year that Ferrari of Los Gatos went, attendees couldn't wait to see what Brian and his team would bring. It was usually a handful of classic cars, but 1989 was different. Ferrari of Los Gatos had about 40 cars to sell, and Dean Kruse gave Ferrari of Los Gatos its own tent, something he'd never done before and probably never since.

A crowd gathered whenever the Ferrari Peterbilt truck pulled up next to the tent. They couldn't wait to get the first glimpse of the cars when the rear doors swung open. Ferrari of Los Gatos created more excitement than anyone or anything else. That probably explains why Brian was the only dealer with his own tent and the only one allowed to hire an independent auctioneer. The regular auctioneers were good, but none achieved the results Brian's auctioneer did. Other dealers begged Brian to use the Ferrari of Los Gatos auctioneer, and he gladly accommodated them. "Sure, you work out a deal directly with him. There's no need for me to be involved." He realized that higher prices would drive the market up for other cars as well. And some of those other cars were sitting on his lot in Los Gatos, waiting to be sold. Brian also believed anything good for the car market was good for everyone. As President John Kennedy once said, "A rising tide lifts all boats."

And the auctions weren't just about cars. Brian would bring a van full of Ferrari of Los Gatos accessories. "I can't remember a time at Kruse or Barrett-Jackson that we didn't sell out of all the T-shirts and license plate frames we brought. We packed that van 'til there was only room for the driver, and we still ran out before the end of the auction." The cars from those auction days have gone up in value, some by millions of dollars, but the license plate frames have done pretty well too. Today, they're hard to find, but an occasional set shows up on eBay for up to $200. That would be about a 2,000 percent gain if you bought one at the auction.

Brian reflects on that year as hard to believe. "I think every one of those 40 cars were sold before they went across the block."

The introduction of the F40 marked the last car Enzo designed, and it became a celebration of the man and the marque.

Supply and demand kicked in for Enzo's last creation, and Ferrari enthusiasts seemed willing to pay anything to own one. In October 1990, the Detroit *Weekly World News* reported that car dealer Dan Anderson bought an F40 from a West Coast Ferrari dealer for more than $1 million and sold it for more. Bob Schneider, the owner of The Sports Car Exchange, Michigan's only authorized Ferrari dealer at the time, said he was selling F40s for between $1.3 and $1.5 million after paying the Ferrari factory about $400,000 for the car. It seems Ferrari of Los Gatos had established the market price for Michigan as well.

Brian received calls daily from people looking for an F40, and all he could do was add them to a waiting list. One of those calls came from an entertainment agent.

"My client is Rod Stewart. He'll be performing a concert at Shoreline Amphitheatre in Mountain View. It's part of his Out of Order world tour. He's looking for a Ferrari, and we heard if anyone could locate one, it would be you."

"Sure, what model is he looking for?" Brian usually got right to the point, no chitchat.

"It's called F40."

"Well, that's not going to be so easy. The F40 is the latest Ferrari to come out of the factory, the last model Mr. Ferrari was involved in, and it's on allocation from the factory. Each dealer receives one F40, we already sold ours, and I currently have a long waiting list."

"I know Mr. Stewart would love to be on the top of your list, Mr. Burnett. He told me to find the F40 at any price." The agent had uttered two of Brian's favorite words—"any price."

"Let me see what I can do. I'll get back to you."

The Ferrari factory assigned dealer allotments based on volume, and, as the number one dealer, this should have helped Brian. But sometimes, favoritism at the factory trumped how many cars a dealer had purchased in the past. Brian recalled that while Ferrari of Los Gatos may have been the dealer with the highest sales, it wasn't the favorite. "If you didn't cave in to the factory and didn't kiss butt, you could end up with the short end of the stick."

But Brian had a knack for locating cars that were hard to come by, although the F40 posed a unique challenge. Even though demand had dropped off a little, the F40 was still on factory allocation, and he could not just order another one.

Never one to give up, Brian used his network to find an F40, purchased from another dealer, that the owner was willing to sell. He purchased it and had it in the back of the Ferrari of Los Gatos lot the day Rod Stewart stopped by.

It was amazing what Brian could accomplish with just a push-button desk phone.

Rod was ecstatic when he saw the car, even when he heard the price tag of almost $1 million (more than $2.3 million in 2021 dollars). Like a kid with a new toy, he couldn't wait to drive it. He spent part of the day with the excited dealership staff. To show his appreciation, Rod invited Brian and salesman Jack Gordon to his sold-out concert.

Later that afternoon, a stretch limousine pulled up outside Ferrari of Los Gatos. The driver had instructions to take care of Brian, Jack, and their companions for the evening. They all fit comfortably into the limousine and enjoyed drinks and snacks on the way to the concert. When they arrived at Shoreline, officials directed the limousine to the VIP entrance gate. When Brian and the group got out of the car, escorts took them to front-row seats, avoiding the 12,879 other people in attendance.

The Ferrari of Los Gatos team enjoyed the concert immensely, especially when Rod smiled, pointed toward them, and gave the group a wink.

And the evening didn't end after the concert did. The limousine drove to the iconic Garden Court Hotel in Palo Alto, where Rod had reserved suites for them. Brian still talks about it today. "That was an evening I will never forget."

Finding the F40 for Rod strengthened Brian's already strong reputation for being able to find any car anytime. His success came partly from the belief that if he set his mind to something, it would happen. Like Bill Harrah, he didn't like being told no or that something was impossible. If Brian wanted something done, it would get done, no matter what obstacles lined his path.

Ferrari of Los Gatos sold 10 F40s, even though the factory shipped only six to the dealership. Brian used his resources to find four more F40s purchased by owners who wanted to sell them for a quick profit. If the numbers made sense, Brian jumped on them. This made his cost go up, but in total, Ferrari of Los Gatos still made a profit of more than $4 million (about $9 million in 2021 dollars) on F40 cars.

In 1995, Ferrari celebrated its 50th anniversary by introducing the F50. The car's 65-degree V-12 engine was a road-modified version of the 1990 Ferrari 641 Formula One car. The F50 engine had five valves per cylinder and turned out 520 horsepower and a top speed of 202 mph. To keep the weight down, the car used a puncture-resistant fuel bag rather than a traditional tank and had no power steering or power brakes, no anti-lock braking system, and windup windows. Former Ferrari President Luca di Montezemolo said the F50 was "the first and last Formula One car with two seats." The factory built 349 of these, and 55 were shipped to the United States.

Anticipation of the F50 was enormous, and Ferrari was concerned that U.S. customers might flip them for a quick profit, as some had done when the F40 was introduced. Ferrari North America hatched a plan to beat potential speculators: F50s would not be sold to anyone in the United States. Those individuals lucky enough to be selected by Ferrari were required to make a $240,000 deposit followed by 24 monthly payments of $5,600 and an additional $150,000 after that in order to take full ownership of the car. It took a total of $524,400 plus taxes for the privilege to lease and then own an F50.

The plan seemed to work because F50 prices didn't skyrocket immediately like F40 prices did in 1988. Or was the reason because Enzo wasn't around anymore to help develop the F50?

Brian was buying cars at a feverish pace now, and the factory had a hard time catching up. So, while Rueben was busy picking up and dropping off cars, Brian was busy buying and selling them from anywhere he could find them. Demand was so high that vehicles could be sold before they even arrived at Ferrari of Los Gatos.

No matter what Brian bought, it seemed like he could make a profit. His minimum profit was around $5,000, but sometimes he'd hit the jackpot, and a hard-to-find classic would bring in hundreds of thousands of dollars.

The only limitation was finding the money to pay for the used cars he purchased on the open market. Brian needed time to sell them, and traditional lenders were reluctant to finance them. Moreover, bankers weren't about to lend money on cars that might go down in value as they sat on a dealer's lot.

Sometimes, success can spoil a good thing, and Brian was about to find out how.

CHAPTER THIRTEEN

Treachery Is Everywhere

(1991)

FLOORING IS ESSENTIAL TO A CAR DEALER, AND THE TERM DOESN'T refer to the part of the showroom where customers walk. Instead, it's a term used for financing a car from the time of purchase until the dealer sells it. Most dealers floor new vehicles purchased from the manufacturer and use their own money to finance used car trade-ins.

Brian followed that business model until the day his ex-banker, Bill Winterhalder, called.

"Brian, remember when I left County Bank in Santa Cruz and started working at Al Cheney Ford?"

"Yes."

"Well, I bought the dealership with the Elward brothers, Mike and Mark, and we changed the name to North Bay Ford."

Having been the Ferrari of Los Gatos banker for years, Bill knew Brian bought and sold used cars and sometimes struggled to find the cash to finance them. He also knew Brian didn't operate like other dealers and liked being different.

"I figured you might still be looking for financing, so my partners and I wanted to talk to you about that."

"Sure, let's get together and talk."

Brian recalled meeting with Bill. "At first I thought he was kidding. He said I could tap into his Ford Motor Credit loan if he could make a little side money. He said they would floor Ferraris or other classic cars and just pass on the interest charged by Ford. When I asked him what's

133

in it for you guys, he said, 'We'll be happy if you just slide us $1,000 per car.'"

Brian thought this would work. He recalled thinking this could be the way to grow the business and increase his profit.

"My ex-banker knew what we were doing in Los Gatos and wanted in on the action. We were selling about 25 to 30 cars a month, and he figured his dealership could pocket an extra $25,000 a month. At that time, for a Ford store, that was a lot of money."

When something seems too good to be true, it probably is.

Bill explained to Brian that the only way this would fly was if Ford Motor credit thought North Bay Ford was part owner in Ferrari of Los Gatos. The paperwork for making the loans would have to be in the name of North Bay Ford, and if they weren't owners in the cars being floored, Ford would not advance funds to them.

"I'm not sure how to make that work. I'm not going to sell the dealership. Things are going pretty good."

"Okay, how about an option."

"What do you mean?"

"You give us an option to buy part of Ferrari of Los Gatos if certain things take place. They can be things you have total control over, and you just make sure they never happen. We already checked with Ford, and they agreed an option would allow us to floor cars for you."

Brian needed financial help and was willing to take on unusual terms and conditions to get it. He believed that having the Ford Motor credit line available would provide the needed financial support, and he'd make sure they never got the dealership. He was willing to do whatever it took, even if it meant letting them have part of the dealership.

Brian wasn't sure whether Winterhalder and the Elwards were scheming to get the dealership or just wanted to make the side fee. However, he didn't really care. "I just told Bill how much I needed to buy a car and sent him the information and title. What North Bay Ford did, how they did it, and what they said was between them and Ford Motor Credit. North Bay Ford did all the paperwork, and I never signed anything. How much was borrowed or where the money ended up, I never knew. As long as I got what was needed to buy the car, I was happy."

Brian's retired friend Chuck Hill knew the Elward brothers as well and enjoyed picking up and dropping off the documents just to have something to do. "Chuck used to walk into my office almost weekly and say, 'Do you have the juice for the boys?'"

The new flooring arrangement was a dream come true—everyone prospered. It provided unlimited capital for Brian, and he covered the $1,000 fee from the profit made on each car's sale. For the Ford dealers, the extra money they made from the fees helped support their dealership. All seemed well.

Flooring used cars was pretty much unheard of at other dealers. But for Brian, it was just another differentiator, and being different had created success at Ferrari of Los Gatos from day one. "Sometimes, we made more money on one car than other dealers would make in a month," Brian would say. "I mean, they believed it, but they couldn't believe it." Brian figured buying a few extra cars and putting them on the lot for sale would make the business do even better.

"It was the biggest mistake of my life."

Hindsight is 20/20.

At first, the plan worked. The cars increased in value, and customers were buying them as fast as Brian could find them. And they didn't stay on the lot very long or were sold before they made it there at all. The business was growing rapidly, and Brian knew it was the Ford Motor flooring that made it possible. So when one classic car made a $100,000 profit, he decided to show his appreciation by giving the Ford dealers a $10,000 bonus.

His goodwill gesture backfired.

The Ford dealers reasoned that if he could afford to give them 10 times their usual fee, they were probably leaving money on the table. On review, they discovered the dealership was making more money than they realized. The Ford dealers decided that Ferrari of Los Gatos should pay more all the time, not just when Brian felt like being generous. Overnight, their fees increased—a lot. The average transaction cost went up

10 times. For an expensive car like the Ferrari F40, they would charge Brian 20 times more.

The higher fees may have made more money for the Ford dealer, but it was temporary. Their greed and ego would come back to haunt them when market conditions changed.

Brian recalled the incredible amount of money the business was making in the late 1980s and how it blinded him. "Things were going along fine. Winterhalder and the Elward brothers were happy with the fees, and I was happy to have the financing available. I called to let them know I'd found a rare Ferrari California Spyder sitting in a body shop in Santa Barbara. The owner of the car wanted it restored and was mad that it had been sitting there for years. I would have to pay him $300,000 to get it, but I knew it was worth it. I told Bill that if they floored the car, I'd let their body shop do the restoration, pay them a $5,000 fee, and 10 percent of the profit when it sold. They jumped at the opportunity, and that was the first big car we did together. Their body shop did an incredible job, completing the restoration in 90 days; I made a profit of $400,000, paid them their $5,000 fee, and gave them another $40,000, representing 10 percent of the profit. Not realizing it at the time, I had repeated the biggest mistake of my life all over again."

Brian found another car in a similar situation. This time, it was a 1966 Ferrari 275 GTB Alloy Long Nose. When he brought the deal to the Ford dealers, they said, "Sure, but this time our fee is $50,000." Brian would be making enough money to cover the hefty fee, and without any other option, he agreed. As he turned to leave, they added, "Oh, and don't forget, we want to share in the profits like last time too." Normally, Brian would have said, "No way," but he was struggling to keep enough cash coming in to continue buying cars and cover expenses. He didn't see any other alternative.

"Before I knew it, they were gouging my eyes," said Brian.

Like a roller-coaster ride climbing to the top, Brian couldn't get off. Some of the big cars sold with trade-ins, and the cash he received covered the interest to Ford Motors, along with the Ford dealers' fee, but left the flooring loan unpaid. After that, the only profit was the car's value sitting out on the lot, still floored by Ford.

The ex-banker and his partners were milking the place and pulling it down. Brian was caught with many cars purchased with Ford flooring, they weren't selling, and their value was falling.

One of the reasons car values were dropping was that Silicon Valley had entered a recession. Boom and bust economic periods are part of the electronics industry that fueled the local economy, and 1991 ended up being a bust year.

On November 29, 1991, the South Jersey *Courier-Post* published an article titled "Silicon Valley Shuts Down to Cut Costs." It explained how well-known Silicon Valley high-tech companies were sending workers home for the holidays so the businesses could trim their costs. Gavin Bourne, a spokesman for Chips & Technologies, Inc., said, "This is the first year we're telling people to stay home." As a result, the company closed for three weeks over the winter holiday period. "We thought this was better than more layoffs."

Several other companies told employees to take vacation time Monday through Wednesday during Thanksgiving week or else forgo pay. For example, IBM announced it would eliminate 20,000 jobs globally and asked workers to stay home between Christmas and New Year's. This was the first time the 2,000-employee Silicon Valley branch of IBM had a Christmas closing.

Silicon Valley companies were doing everything they could to cut costs without losing people.

This recession reminded people of the downturn that took place five years earlier. That slowdown had been caused by three reasons. First, the initial demand for personal computers had been filled. Second, an excessive inventory buildup of electronic components drove prices down. Finally, foreign competition cut into Silicon Valley's market share. Thirty-five percent of the local factory and research space was vacant, and 28,000 jobs were lost.

An article appeared in the San Jose *Mercury News* titled "The Thrill Is Gone: Valley Adapts to High-Tech Slump." It described Silicon Valley learning to live with disappointment for the first time with no relief in sight. The newspaper staff writers Pete Carey and Jonathan Eig wrote, "Some corporations no longer throw corporate bashes to mark the end of another week, freewheelers have returned Ferraris purchased just months ago, and the flourishing bar scene has faded."

The article pointed to the signs of changing times visible on dealership lots, where flashy cars were sold, and in bars and restaurants, where million-dollar deals were once made.

The newspaper interviewed Brian and published his comments in the article.

"We are getting a few of the electronics people that didn't do so well wanting to sell their cars," says Brian Burnett, president of Ferrari of Los Gatos. "As we talk to them, they are nervous that business hasn't come back yet. And a lot who were going to buy cars are not now."

Burnett speculates some of those postponing purchases "don't want to be flaunting a new Ferrari in front of people they are laying off."

Joe Orlando, a bartender at Pedro's Restaurant and Cantina located off Highway 101 in Santa Clara, was interviewed at 4:30 p.m. in an empty bar. Free nachos and tacos sat untouched.

He told how a few years earlier, between 4 and 5 p.m., it was standing room only. "People would come in at 12 and stay for hours discussing million-dollar deals regularly."

"Now, the only time business booms is when there's a layoff," according to Paul Witthar, Pedro's general manager. "On these Black Wednesdays and Thursdays, all of a sudden, we've got a full bar."

Regardless of who was right or wrong, it pointed out that Silicon Valley, once known for its Ferrari-driving entrepreneurs, extravagant Christmas parties, afternoon beer bashes, and desk-side massages, had definitely toned down.

During the recovery years between the two recessions, Brian's success had seduced him into thinking he was invincible and that the business could take care of itself. As a result, he lost focus when Ferrari of Los Gatos needed him the most. He couldn't see that others were positioning themselves to try to take away the company he'd built.

Greed and ego reared their ugly heads, and the loans outstanding were more than the value of the cars sitting on the lot at Ferrari of Los

Gatos. Brian knew the deal with North Bay Ford and Ford Motor Credit could blow up at any time, and it wasn't going to be pretty.

Sometimes it's hard to determine who your true enemy is. Unfortunately, Brian was about to find out he had more than one.

CHAPTER FOURTEEN

The New Regime

(1993)

ENZO FERRARI DIED ON AUGUST 17, 1988, AND FOR THE NEXT FIVE years, the company he'd founded 41 years earlier fell into disarray. The legendary company was in shambles. No new leader emerged, and no one took responsibility for anything.

When it came to what Ferrari was best known for, Formula One racing, the team hit an all-time low with Enzo gone. Ferrari drivers had won eight world racing championships by 1988, but without Enzo around, 12 years would pass before a Ferrari driver won a world championship title again.

For the first time, the factory in Maranello had unsold cars lined up on their lot, and management was struggling. It was chaotic, and the Italians around Maranello said they could feel it.

For Brian and Ferrari of Los Gatos, the perfect storm was brewing, but he did not see it coming.

Over the years, Brian accomplished what Enzo's management team said couldn't be done. Ferrari's marketing mavens thought Americans would never understand or appreciate his car's value and, therefore, would never pay the price. Through Ferrari of Los Gatos, Brian proved them wrong. He'd found a way to sell Ferraris to the average American, sold more of them than anyone else, and made the North American market a big success for the Italian carmaker. And along the way, he helped other Ferrari dealers become successful as well.

But good times don't last forever.

Giovanni Agnelli, the leader of Ferrari's controlling shareholder, Fiat, formed a new management team. He appointed Luca Cordero di Montezemolo as president of Ferrari. Montezemolo had worked for Enzo in the 1970s and wanted to bring back the original Ferrari principles: to race and win in Formula One and produce exclusive, high-performance road machines. So he focused on that and left the fate of North American dealers in the hands of others.

The others included Gian Longinotti-Buitoni, president and CEO of Ferrari North America. In June 1993, Ferrari reported sales of fewer than 500 cars in the United States, most of them in Northern California. Buitoni knew most of the new Ferraris were being sold through Ferrari of Los Gatos but had no idea how many used Ferraris and other classic cars the dealership sold. When he learned a little more about what was taking place on that street corner in Los Gatos, he joined the list of people who wanted the stone. His first move was to acquire the San Francisco Ferrari dealership, close it, and move the business to a new company-owned store in Mill Valley. Unfortunately, the San Francisco dealership wasn't in San Francisco anymore but over the Golden Gate Bridge in Marin County.

Ferrari now had a company-owned store in the hottest market in North America.

Brian remembers those difficult years.

"The Marin County store became the base of operations for Ferrari North America, and they used it to launch attacks against other dealers. There are times when a business or a government seems to care about two things only—power and money. As far as the people that did the work to make them grow and become successful—they don't care. So if it's beneficial to step on those people, they step on them."

Buitoni told Brian he couldn't understand how Ferrari of Los Gatos sold more than his Mill Valley dealership. After all, Ferrari invested a lot of money to buy the dealership and build a beautiful new store. And he didn't understand how Brian was so successful selling those big used cars. Trying to figure it out, he phoned and visited Brian frequently.

"How do you do this? And how do you sell these old used cars?"

"I don't know exactly how to explain this to you," Brian told him. "You have to know cars, and you have to like cars. You have to believe in the older Ferraris as well as the new Ferrari models."

Although he didn't tell Buitoni, at the time, those new Ferraris were terrible, and selling them was a challenge. They didn't compete well with Porsche or Mercedes. Because of that, Ferrari of Los Gatos sold lots of older Ferrari models—people liked them.

It turned out that both men would be attending the first annual Father's Day Rodeo Drive Concours d'Elegance in Beverly Hills a few weeks later. Buitoni told Brian, "I will look for you at the Concours. Our CEO, Luca di Montezemolo, will be there to introduce the new Ferrari 348 Spyder."

Knowing that Ferrari would be bringing new models to the show, Brian and his staff brought older models. The group stayed at the Beverly Hilton and met at the hotel bar nightly. After a day of hobnobbing with celebrities and Ferrari executives on Rodeo Drive, Buitoni decided to visit Brian and his crew. He knew they'd be at the hotel bar and headed there to meet with them.

After saying hello to the group, he asked to speak with Brian privately. The two men walked across the room to a balcony overlooking Beverly Hills. As the largest and most successful dealer in the United States and Canada, it wasn't surprising that Buitoni would talk to Brian first about his plans for North America.

"Buitoni told me he'd be making some changes in the way things work and wanted to know who's going to go along and work with him. I asked him what exactly he was talking about?"

"We plan to buy out dealers. We will buy out smaller dealers and close them. They aren't selling much anyway. Those dealers are successful because they have bigger lines to sell." He was referring to the fact that to many dealers, the Ferrari franchise was a sideline to their primary business selling BMWs, Chevys, and Fords.

"Buitoni asked me to help get rid of these guys. I asked him, 'How can I help you do that?' He told me I should act like, you know, things are getting grim, and it's not going to be a good franchise business anymore.

He said if they call you, you're going to need to convince them that it's probably a good idea to sell back to Ferrari."

Buitoni knew that the other dealers had a great deal of respect for Brian because he had helped them out over the years. The conversation continued.

"Luigi, these people are my friends. I'm not doing that. I will not backstab people I care about. They aren't bothering anything by having their dealerships."

"Brian, I would advise you to work with me. Help me get rid of these guys and tell them, you know, whatever. Talk to them and convince them to go along with us, and we will take care of you."

"I'm not gonna screw over these people. We've traveled together and have become friends. I want them to be successful. I don't want to hurt them."

"You don't understand what I'm trying to do."

"Well, I think I do, and I don't like it."

Brian almost told him that he didn't like him either but thought that might be going a little too far.

At the time, things were going well. They were not the best times Brian had experienced, but even so, he couldn't understand why Ferrari would want to do this. Buitoni said the locations they wanted to close weren't necessary. Brian figured what he really meant was he wanted to run the other dealers' sales through his Mill Valley company-owned store.

And Buitoni never mentioned closing successful dealerships like Beverly Hills, San Diego, New York, Detroit, Houston, or Ferrari of Los Gatos. Brian could tell they wanted to keep those profitable dealers for themselves, and they'd do that by converting them to company-owned stores.

"Buitoni told me that if I went along with their plan, I'd receive a position within Ferrari North America, and they'd take care of me in the future. I told him, 'Luigi, that's not gonna happen.'

"He continued to tell me how serious he was and that the people that worked with him would survive and enjoy the rest of their tenure with Ferrari. The people who didn't work with him would be gone.

"I didn't respond, and Buitoni turned, walked back to the bar, and started talking with the others as if he'd never left."

After returning to Los Gatos, Brian learned that one or two small dealers had sold out to Ferrari. He figured they didn't give a damn because they weren't making any money off the cars anyhow. For Brian and several other dealers, it was their livelihood. In some cases, it was their life.

It seemed like Buitoni forgot about Ferrari of Los Gatos. He never called or visited after the meeting in Beverly Hills, and Brian was operating the dealership the same way he had for years. He had no idea what Buitoni was up to but should have tried to figure it out.

A few months passed since Brian and Buitoni had met when a well-dressed older gentleman walked into the dealership. The visitor looked like he'd just stepped out of a clothing store in England or Scotland. Every inch of his suit was crisp and pressed. He asked for Brian.

"My name is Michael Jackling, and I've been sent here by Ferrari. I want to talk with you about why they hired me. Perhaps we could speak privately in your office?"

Brian nodded, and they walked into his office. He closed the door, and Jackling got right to the point.

"Ferrari has hired me to buy back dealerships. I have prior experience doing this for Jaguar."

Brian knew the story and realized he was sitting across from "the henchman," the nickname Jackling was given by the Jaguar dealers years ago. Brian didn't comment right away, so Jackling repeated himself.

"Ferrari has decided to buy your dealership. They want to buy you out."

Brian thought, *this guy can't pull anything over on me*, and responded, "That's great because, to be honest with you, I'm tired of this crap. I've got a guy that wants to buy the place right now, but it would be a lot easier to sell it to you guys. So, let's make a deal."

Jackling responded by taking out a notepad, writing down a number, and sliding the paper across the desk.

"That's what we are paying."

Brian glanced down at the paper.

It read $978,000.

Brian didn't laugh in Jackling's face, but he sure felt like it. He knew Monterey and a couple of other smaller dealerships had been bought out and figured they had probably given in to Ferrari.

"Well, no, that's not what you're paying. That may be what you want to pay, but this place is worth a little more than that. I've made more than that on one car."

Jackling was taken aback by Brian's response.

"Well, if you don't do as Ferrari asks, how are you going to get any cars? Ferrari has no incentive to sell you any cars unless you go along with our plan."

"Well, we have franchise dealer laws here in California, and as long as I can pay for the cars, you know the law says you have to send them to me."

The two men talked for the better part of an hour. Jackling spoke in parables to make his points. He told Brian how the Vatican in Rome rang its bells for only one nonreligious reason—when Ferrari won a race. He explained how having this much power and influence meant you could do things your way. He reminded Brian that the most prominent companies in the world had not been able to defeat Ferrari. Ford, for example, had a signed contract to buy Ferrari, but it got torn up when Mr. Ferrari didn't like what he heard. He threw in that the only reason Ford won Le Mans was that one Ferrari crashed and the other one broke down. He insisted Ferrari lost just because they had bad luck that weekend. Brian knew that Ford had won Le Mans three years in a row but let it go.

"Brian, you seem like a nice guy. We know you do great business here, which is one reason Ferrari wants the store. Everyone in the business has something to say about Ferrari of Los Gatos. Not always something good, but they talk about you much more than any other dealer."

"Well, we're not here to impress anybody. We just want to sell cars."

"Brian, we want to buy the stores that do the best, and we don't want 50 dealers in the U.S. anymore. We will close small unprofitable dealers and move others to new locations. Los Gatos is not the right place to have this store anyhow. It should be in Menlo Park or Atherton, where the wealthy people are."

Brian thought this guy doesn't know what he's talking about. Like there are no rich people here. "Look, Mr. Jackling, it wouldn't matter if this store was up in the hillside community of Redwood Estates. People come because of the cars, not the location."

Brian had enough and decided to play his cards.

"I think what I'll do right now is pick up the phone and see what I can sell it for. Would you like to listen?"

Jackling nodded.

Brian called the Honda dealer that had shown interest in buying the dealership in the past.

"Tom, are you still interested in buying this place?" He made sure to hold the phone out so Jackling could hear the answer.

"Hell yes I am."

"The price is $4 million."

"I'll be there with a check in the morning if you're serious."

"I'll get back to you, Tom."

Brian hung up the phone, looked Jackling in the eyes, and shrugged his shoulders.

Jackling stood up to leave and then turned back.

"Let me tell you something, Brian. At the end of the day, Ferrari will own this dealership, and you won't."

Brian would never speak to Jackling again.

Over time, Brian would fight many battles with Ferrari learning what he had sensed: right or wrong, the company doesn't lose, ever.

But for now, being the number one dealer went to Brian's head. He thought the business could run on autopilot and figured his staff would handle it. Maybe he was going through a little middle-aged craziness as well, but for some reason, he was doing foolish things, not only at work but in all aspects of his life.

Leaving the day-to-day operations to his staff, Brian stopped spending time at the dealership. Unfortunately, he didn't realize the threats made by Buitoni and Jackling were starting to materialize.

Buitoni knew cars from Italy arrived at the port in Los Angeles and sat there for several weeks before being sent to the dealers. He had access to everyone's records regarding which dealer ordered which car. He knew Ferrari of Los Gatos got more cars than the factory allocated to an individual dealer. He didn't know why but was determined to find out.

Brian had become friends with the woman who managed the Ferrari port-of-entry office in Los Angeles. She was responsible for receiving the cars and taking care of any damage or flaws before they went to dealers. If a dealer ever said they didn't want a particular vehicle, she would automatically call Ferrari of Los Gatos. Taking almost every car that became available helped her move cars out of the port warehouse.

"I would get first choice on the cars other dealers didn't take. And I never said no; whether I wanted them or not, I took them. I did this because I knew that someday they would be harder to get."

Taking cars the port manager didn't have a home for was part of the reason Ferrari of Los Gatos was successful. It got Brian to the top of the list every time a new car came in. Buitoni probably wanted to control where the cars went and the port manager got reassigned to another job. Suddenly, there were no more phone calls to Ferrari of Los Gatos about unwanted cars.

Buitoni knew the name of every new car customer at Ferrari of Los Gatos because he had access to factory sales records. Armed with that information, he decided to try to move those orders to the company-owned store.

Customers told Brian that while they wanted to buy their car from him, the Mill Valley store had called and said that they'd get it a lot faster if they switched their order. Even longtime loyal customers said, "I don't want to do this, but I want my car. Please give me my deposit back."

Cash flow became a problem for Ferrari of Los Gatos, especially when the cars sold were not delivered. In the ordinary course of business, Ferrari of Los Gatos took deposits on new vehicles, set a delivery date, and waited to collect the balance of the total price when the car was delivered. Without notice, delivery dates started to slip. In the past, late deliveries were unusual. It got worse and worse, and Brian could not get a straight answer from the factory about when the cars he'd ordered would arrive. He recalled what Jackling had said. "Well, if you don't do as Ferrari asks, how are you going to get any cars? Ferrari has no incentive to sell you any cars unless you go along with our plan."

With only customer deposits on new vehicles coming in, Brian had to use that money to offset the cash drain caused by the nondelivery of cars he'd sold. Brian knew this was only a temporary solution, but he had no other choice. He'd correct everything once the factory delivered the vehicles.

Unfortunately, it was a recipe for disaster. Ferrari of Los Gatos was under attack.

Other unusual things started happening as well. For example, every other year, Ferrari would publish a new service and warranty parts book. Included with the part numbers and descriptions would be new prices. Since 1976, prices for parts had increased between 5 and 15 percent when the parts book was issued. The dealers didn't like it but realized that prices rose over time just like the cars they bought. Or did they?

Brian thought it was strange that, for the first time, the parts book showed up with price decreases. The cars weren't going down in price. Why would the parts? He hadn't connected the dots yet but would realize later this was no coincidence. When a dealership was closed or taken over by the factory, Ferrari had to pay the dealer for the inventory of spare parts and any special tools and equipment. If parts prices went down, Ferrari would have less to pay when they bought out the dealerships and repurchased the parts.

Brian also discovered that some international locations previously covered by North American dealers were now being supplied directly by the factory. When the factory sold direct, it reduced the number of cars available for the U.S. market. That also reduced the profitability of the North American dealers. Yet the company-owned store in Mill Valley always had plenty of vehicles in stock, and if they didn't have the model or color a customer wanted, they could get it from the factory promptly.

To top it off, Brian was not himself. Usually, if anyone tried to use tactics like this against him, he would not let them get away with it. He remembered feeling stifled. "For some reason, I just let them beat the crap out of me. I don't know what was going on, but I was in a tailspin at that time."

Not only had Brian spent about $4 million trying to keep Ferrari of Los Gatos alive, but he also ended up neglecting his marriage during the fight against Ferrari. He recalled how difficult life became at that time. "I was certainly not a very nice person to live with while all this was going on."

Next, customers started complaining about service. They couldn't understand what was taking so long and why their cars weren't ready. They didn't know that the factory never shipped the service parts that Ferrari of Los Gatos had ordered. Not shipping service parts was another tactic used by Ferrari to undermine the dealership. Next, they claimed Ferrari of Los Gatos was a problem dealer that could no longer provide timely service to their customers.

"It was like a run on a bank," Brian recalled. "Every customer wanted their deposits back." Brian was in survival mode and trying to save the business.

"I was no day at the beach either but didn't have the customers' money anymore and couldn't return their deposits. Ferrari tried to take advantage of the situation and make me look like the bad guy."

Pieces of the puzzle started fitting together, but Brian's time was running out.

The assaults from Buitoni and the Mill Valley factory store hurt Brian. Then, when the dealership took deposits on cars that didn't get delivered, Ferrari had another opportunity to undermine Brian even more.

It wasn't long before Brian's sales staff started wondering how long they'd have a job. The dealership was on the ropes, and Buitoni hired a Ferrari of Los Gatos team member to work at the company store. "Buitoni wanted to learn my secret of success and figured he'd understand that from the Ferrari of Los Gatos sales staff he hired, plus he'd get my contact list of classic car collectors that had taken years to develop."

In the middle of this barrage of attacks, Brian remembers being mentally and physically exhausted. "I felt defeated and began realizing that I couldn't beat these guys." He'd been the best of the best for a long time, but he'd lost his A-game. His world was unraveling, and he'd lost control of his business, marriage, and family.

He awoke one morning and sat on the edge of his bed. Then, gazing into nowhere, he said out loud, "I'm done."

But the old Brian was in there somewhere, the one who never gave up no matter what obstacle lay in his path. He had to dig deep but eventually found him.

Brian reached for the phone.

CHAPTER FIFTEEN

I'm Back—All Over Again

(1993)

"You still want the dealership?"

"Hell, yeah, I want it."

"It's still 4 million bucks."

"I own it."

Tom Roulette, a wealthy Silicon Valley car dealer who owned a Honda and a Chevy store, was the person Brian had contacted a few months earlier when Michael Jackling made Ferrari's $978,000 offer. At that time, Tom had said he'd buy the dealership for $4 million, and he was still interested now.

"Remember, Ferrari's trying to force me to sell to them."

"Let's meet with our attorney and see about that."

Later that day, Brian met with Tom and Bill Winterhalder of North Bay Ford at the law offices of Mike Morrisey, an attorney they had all used previously. Mike had successfully defeated Honda in a lawsuit against Tom and successfully helped North Bay Ford but struggled to help Brian against Ferrari.

Tom told Brian that Bill Winterhalder and the Elward brothers were partners and would continue financing Ferrari of Los Gatos through Ford Motor Credit.

Mike listened to what everyone wanted and said he could write a contract to seal the deal. Unsure about some of the terms and conditions, Brian asked to speak with Mike in private.

"Mike, I'm concerned about how this is going to work. I don't want this dealership with all the debts getting back on me. What happens if Tom or North Bay wants out?"

"You've got to turn it over to them Brian. Tom's a good operator and knows how to sell cars, and Bill has the flooring needed through Ford Motor Credit. Together they can make this work. Sign the deal and then take some time to clear your head and do whatever you want." Unable to see any other option and looking forward to some time away from the mess, Brian agreed.

When they rejoined Tom and Bill, Brian reminded them what Jackling had said regarding selling to anyone other than Ferrari. "Tom, remember what they told me, 'You don't have a choice because we will never approve anyone else.'"

"You know what Brian? That's against the law. The law reads you cannot unreasonably withhold the transfer of a franchise to a qualified person." And Tom was more than qualified.

As if he didn't remember a word Brian had said in private, Mike suggested wording in the contract to protect Tom if Ferrari did not approve him. Brian refused. "I've told you exactly what Ferrari said to me. You've said it's not a concern because of the law, and I need to know I'm out, no matter what happens between you and Ferrari."

Mike looked at Tom with a glance that suggested the wording should be in, but Tom said, "You're right Brian, they have no choice. So, screw them. I'll take 'em to the wall."

Brian didn't realize that no one was negotiating with him on anything. He also didn't notice how quickly the attorney's position had flipped. Mike repeated what Tom had said: "Yeah, we'll take 'em to the wall."

On signing the contract, Brian received a down payment of $400,000. Mike told Brian that he should give Tom something as security for the deposit. While this was not customary in standard purchase agreements, Brian was not thinking clearly and agreed. And he should not have been using the same attorney who represented Tom and Bill, especially since Mike had made Tom a lot of money defeating Honda.

Brian had no money, so Mike suggested using other assets, like his classic cars and speedboat, to secure the down payment. Unfortunately, Brian didn't realize the down payment should be nonrefundable and unsecured. It was the attorney's job to advise Brian against this, but that never took place.

The cars and boat were not worth the total $400,000, so Brian pledged several Rolex watches he'd purchased or received as gifts. He was a desperate man, trying to get out of a bad situation, and he wasn't thinking like a businessman. He also didn't see that Tom and North Bay Ford had nothing to lose. If either changed their mind, Tom could get his $400,000 back by selling Brian's security. In the meantime, Tom and North Bay Ford would have complete operating control of Ferrari of Los Gatos.

Brian proceeded, signed the contract, and felt somewhat vindicated. Maybe he could pay back the people he owed deposits to and move on to the next phase of his life with this deal. After all, that had always been his goal.

The $400,000 went into the dealership to pay the sales staff, delinquent rent, past-due operating expenses, and return some customer deposits. But what seemed like a lot of money disappeared quickly.

Tom and Bill took over responsibility for operating the dealership, and Brian felt as if they had lifted the weight of the world from his shoulders. Even so, it was hard adjusting to not running the dealership he'd been responsible for during the past 13 years. "I needed some time to lick my wounds. So, I didn't do anything but plan how I would pay off the rest of my debts and start over again."

After a few months, Brian figured the balance due would get paid any day. He knew Tom would deduct the number of outstanding loans owed Ford Motor Credit from the final payment. That was part of the original agreement. So Brian was to get whatever was left. Tom had estimated that would be around $1 million.

Instead, he was surprised one morning when his phone rang and he heard his office manager's voice.

"Brian, you better get down here right away. Tom's gone, and there's no money in the bank. I'm not sure what to do."

"What do you mean, Tom's gone?"

"He gave me his keys and said he's not going to buy the store. He said something about Ferrari not approving him as a dealer."

"Okay, I'll be right over."

Just when he thought he was out, they pulled him back in.

Brian was in shock and disbelief when he arrived at the dealership and discovered what had happened. Tom had sold cars without paying off the flooring; there were wages, commissions, and other bills to pay; and Tom had cleared out the bank accounts. On top of that, it looked like Brian had lost the cars, boats, and watches he put up as security.

It didn't surprise him that Ferrari disapproved of Tom; he'd been clear on that possibility from the start. And he thought he'd made sure that Ferrari's nonapproval was not a way for Tom to get out of the agreement. Tom and Bill had told the sales staff that the business wasn't viable without new cars from the factory. Then they packed up and left.

Brian thought he was out but found himself faced with no option except to return and save the company. But since the $400,000 deposit he'd received was spent to pay the debts Ferrari of Los Gatos had incurred, there was no money left to operate the business.

On top of the business problems, his marriage ended in divorce, and he had no personal assets anymore. When his ex-wife Tina found out what he was going through, she offered to invest $800,000 of her money into Ferrari of Los Gatos. She believed in Brian and the business and wanted to help save it. She also thought it was a good investment and was looking forward to eventually having part ownership in the new Ferrari of Los Gatos.

Although he desperately needed the money, Brian advised Tina not to do this. He explained it would only postpone the inevitable and told her there was a high risk of losing the money.

She decided to do it anyway.

Brian now had some capital to work with and had to figure out a way out of the unexpected mess. It was a difficult task, and his anger for what Tom and North Bay Ford had done would cloud his judgment.

Flying solo now, Brian tried on his own to turn the business around and save it. He worked hard to sell all the used vehicles he could, tried to get Ferrari to send him new cars, and paid whatever he could to Ford Motor Credit. But no matter what, he couldn't seem to get his head above water. Every time he started to reach the surface, someone or something would push him back down. Most of the time, it was Ferrari.

In full attack mode now, not only were they refusing to ship new cars to fill orders, but they were also attacking the service and repair shop.

Buitoni knew what factory warranty work Ferrari of Los Gatos performed because he monitored service parts ordered by the dealership.

Trucks from the Mill Valley store showed up and drove away with cars in the Los Gatos shop for warranty repair work. The drivers told Ferrari of Los Gatos repair technicians that the factory store was required to do the job, and Brian wasn't around to question or stop them. One time, an expensive F40 model sold by Ferrari of Los Gatos needed a new engine, a job that could run up to $30,000. When Buitoni found out about it, service parts got rerouted to the Mill Valley company store, and a truck came down and grabbed the car.

And not only was Ferrari taking away lucrative warranty work, but they weren't paying Ferrari of Los Gatos for the warranty work that had already been done. Brian's repair shop manager let him know Ferrari had not paid for warranty work in almost three months. Brian immediately called Ferrari of North America, and all they said was, "We don't know what's going on."

Brian blamed Buitoni and Jackling for the situation. If they would ship cars to him, he knew he could fix everything. Part of the problem was that Ferrari knew that as well. "I had deposits for six F50s. If Ferrari had delivered those six cars to me, the profits would have paid everything and everyone. Unfortunately, they wouldn't deliver them because I hadn't agreed to help them with their plan to take over other dealers. They swallowed up those six cars and sold them through the company-owned store. My customers lost their deposits, and eventually, I ended up losing everything I owned."

Brian saw that between the different players, no one wanted him to succeed. But Ferrari seemed to want him to fail the most. After all, they had the most to gain by taking over Ferrari of Los Gatos.

Brian realized that maybe Chuck Hill had been right all along when he said, "Sometimes your true enemy doesn't reveal himself." The friends whom Brian had trusted to help him save Ferrari of Los Gatos, pay off its debts, and start over again might have had a hand in his demise. Was it a coincidence that Roulette, Winterhalder, the Elward brothers, and attorney Morrissey were all trying to help him at the same time? Were they even trying to help him? When the going got tough, they disappeared, leaving Brian trying to figure out how to clean up their mess. And why had Roulette never attempted to negotiate a better price? Brian had thrown out a number, a high number at that: $4 million. Roulette's immediate response had been, "I own it," although car guys usually negotiate. It's part of their DNA.

Brian knew that while Ferrari had taken him to the top, it also pushed him into the abyss of financial failure.

It seemed that everyone wanted the stone.

CHAPTER SIXTEEN

The Aftermath

(1994)

BRIAN WAS STRUGGLING TO MAKE ENDS MEET. HE'D PUT ALL HIS MONEY into the dealership, used the $400,000 deposit he received from Tom Roulette to pay Ferrari of Los Gatos debts, and reluctantly took $800,000 from his ex-wife Tina trying to save the business. The money from Tina was a significant portion of what she'd received in their divorce settlement, but she believed in Brian and wanted to support him. To this day, they are close friends, enjoy spending time together at family functions, and sometimes reminisce about their time together in Camelot.

Having to come back in and operate the dealership after Roulette abandoned it, Brian worked hard to sell any cars he could. Still, the money those sales brought in hardly covered the deficit the business had incurred. He was bleeding cash at an alarming rate. Unfortunately, none of these actions were enough to turn things around.

In July 1994, Ford showed up to do an audit. They compared the list of outstanding vehicle loans to the actual cars on the lot. The purpose of the review was to make sure all the vehicles listed were still on the lot. Unfortunately, the audit disclosed that 19 of the vehicles listed were missing. They'd been sold, and whether it was Ferrari of Los Gatos or the Ford dealer, someone hadn't paid the loan, and Brian knew that meant trouble.

And the hits kept coming. In August, Ferrari decided not to renew the Ferrari of Los Gatos franchise, which created a roadblock for Brian to sell the dealership. A week later, the State of California Department of Motor Vehicles suspended the Ferrari of Los Gatos license to sell cars.

When it rains, it pours, and Brian had a hard time staying focused. "I wasn't the type that usually gives up, but I had nowhere to turn." Based on his inability to see a way out, he filed for Chapter 11 bankruptcy protection.

"I knew that in Chapter 11, you have to pay back what you owe, but you keep going. I knew a lot of people went bankrupt when they had problems. I wanted to save the business, and I wanted to pay back everyone."

Even though the profits for the F50s he'd sold were reduced due to the leasing arrangement, Brian believed that if Ferrari had delivered those cars, he could have continued operating the business and eventually turned things around.

Instead, Ford came and took action on the audit, which had revealed that cars Ferrari of Los Gatos had not yet paid the loan for had been sold. "In the middle of the mess I was in, Ford came in the night and locked the place up with a chain. With liens on specific vehicles only, they had no right to seize the entire dealership—that was against the law. They even sold some cars and kept the proceeds. I remember the judge telling Ford, 'You cannot do this. You guys have a problem.' And he later told Ferrari the same thing. So both Ford and Ferrari were doing everything they could to put me out of business."

Attorneys for the dealership argued that Ford voided any financial agreement between the parties by not giving Ferrari of Los Gatos proper legal notice. The bankruptcy judge agreed. He advised Ford they might have to give the money back and forfeit any claims against the cars they took control of without proper legal authority.

On January 1, 1995, a newspaper article appeared in the *Santa Cruz Sentinel* by staff writer Steve Perez titled, "Loan for Pricey Cars Turns Sour." The article stated that Bill Winterhalder and two other principals of North Bay Ford, brothers Mark and Michael Elward, guaranteed that Ferrari of Los Gatos would repay loans to Ford Motor Credit. In court documents, Ford claimed that both Ferrari of Los Gatos and the owners of North Bay Ford were liable for somewhere between $2 million and $6 million. Those documents spelled out that North Bay guaranteed the loan subject to certain conditions. It was also reported that North Bay

Ford claimed that they were owed $173,000 in trade debt and flooring costs from Ferrari of Los Gatos. Winterhalder and the Elward brothers claimed that they didn't owe anything to Ford Motor Credit and, since Brian never signed any agreement with Ford, believed that he didn't owe them anything either.

On top of the claims by Ford Motor Credit and North Bay Ford, one salesman for Ferrari of Los Gatos filed a claim for $1 million in unpaid commissions. Brian explained why this was absurd. "The F40 had so much demand with limited supply that dealers across the country had them presold. In fact, most dealers told their sales teams there would be no commissions paid to anyone for F40s. They made sales of that model house accounts. I, on the other hand, told my sales staff that if an F40 was assigned to one of their customers, they'd receive a commission, but it would be capped at $25,000 per car. The salesman filing the $1 million claim wanted his full commission, not just the $25,000 on each car he'd been paid."

Ferrari of Los Gatos attorney Wayne Thomas filed a request for a delay in the bankruptcy hearings to give the dealership time to address the various filings by Ferrari, Ford Motor Credit, North Bay Ford, Tom Roulette, employees, and general creditors. Brian received a little breathing room when the bankruptcy court judge ordered a five-month delay in Ferrari of North America's efforts to strip Ferrari of Los Gatos of its dealership franchise. At the same time, the judge reminded Ford Motor Credit they might have overstepped their rights by selling cars without giving Ferrari of Los Gatos proper legal notice.

It was difficult for Brian to know what to do. Ferrari was crushing the dealership from the outside while Winterhalder, the Elwards, and Roulette seemed to be taking it down from the inside. Finally, he realized Ferrari would not let the dealership get sold unless the bankruptcy court ordered it. Brian recalled how devastated he felt at the time. "My original attorney, Michael Morrissey, was missing in action. I hired Wayne Thomas to represent Ferrari of Los Gatos and try to get the mess sorted out." Morrissey had personal issues and sought financial relief under Chapter 7 of the Bankruptcy Code in 1995. Morrissey represented himself, and the bankruptcy court refused to accept some of the documents he submitted. He sued the bankruptcy court, but the U.S. Court of Appeals affirmed a Bankruptcy Appellate Panels decision that Morrissey submitted deficient briefs and excerpts, some of which were incomprehensible. No wonder he'd been unable to properly defend Ferrari of Los Gatos, especially when Ford was on the ropes for not following the proper legal procedure. At one point, it seemed like the judge might rule that Brian had the right to the cars and was not responsible for the loans arranged by Winterhalder and the Elward brothers with Ford Motor Credit. Somehow, that option disappeared.

Disciplinary actions taken by the court included suspending Morrissey's license in October 1997. As a result, he lost eligibility to practice law in California. From 1997 to 2012, his on-again, off-again licensing culminated in becoming ineligible to practice law in California. Nine months later, he was disbarred. As of July 2021, the State of California had not reinstated his license.

Brian realized that he had played a large part in the demise of the business, but without a reliable attorney, it was virtually impossible to overcome the attacks. He continued to try to save the dealership while it was in bankruptcy but never seemed to be able to turn the corner enough to get it going profitably again. "I felt I had failed miserably. I'd taken the best Ferrari dealership in America and tubed the whole thing. Of course, I had a lot to do with the mess it was in, but I still believe I could have made it work if all the other side stuff had not been happening."

And while Ferrari of Los Gatos continued to slip toward a total collapse, he thought about how he had responded to Ferrari. "In the end, I was watching Ferrari destroy the other dealers. Buitoni had warned me, saying that unless I worked with him and helped him get rid of some of these dealers, I'd be on the outside. Maybe protecting the other dealers was the wrong move for me from a personal financial standpoint, but I could never live with myself had I done otherwise. These people were my friends."

Eventually, the bankruptcy court appointed a trustee to run Ferrari of Los Gatos, and Brian had to leave. One night he locked the door, looked around one last time, and never came back.

Over the next three years, bankruptcy trustee Charles Simms ran the business as an absentee owner would. He visited occasionally but did not understand the inner workings of the car business and let the sales staff run the day-to-day operations. That proved to be fatal. The court used its legal leverage to force Ferrari to ship new cars to Ferrari of Los Gatos, but with the trustee offsite, the profits never amounted to enough to turn the business around. It's not unusual that some sales never get recorded without the owner around and the business eventually must be sold. That's what happened with Ferrari of Los Gatos.

In 1998, the bankruptcy court approved the sale of Ferrari of Los Gatos to Symbolic Motor Car Company, Inc., located in La Jolla, California. Ferrari attempted to block the sale based on three points. First, in 1979, a Symbolic business associate had pleaded guilty to the misdemeanor of furnishing a gratuity to a federal employee. Second, in 1982, a relative of Symbolic owner, Marc Chase, had been convicted of selling cocaine and possessing an unregistered firearm. And third, in 1993, another Symbolic business associate had been convicted of misdemeanor battery and fined $125. The court rejected Ferrari's objections, stating that "complaints would have had more force if the misdeeds were not so remote in time and if they bore directly upon the operation of an automobile franchise."

On May 24, 1998, the sale of Ferrari of Los Gatos to Symbolic closed.

Chapter Seventeen

Life without Ferrari

(1995–2000)

Race cars sometimes start a race strong but end up trackside or in the pit area, never to cross the finish line. These cars are listed DNF, meaning "did not finish." Brian was a DNF.

What started as the ride of a lifetime detoured into being convicted of bankruptcy fraud and losing everything. Brian had broken and stretched the rules to survive, and that took him from top to bottom. He never intentionally wanted to cheat or hurt anyone and thought the good times would return, allowing him to repay everyone. His worst mistake was losing focus and trusting friends and associates who wanted what he had. An incurable optimist, he thought that being part of Ferrari could fix anything. But, unfortunately, it was his success that destroyed him and the dealership he created.

The millennium celebrations were a worldwide, coordinated series of events celebrating the end of 1999 and the start of the year 2000. For Brian, it meant the statute of limitations was just around the corner. "The statute of limitations for anyone to do anything to me was about to run out. Ever since I'd lost the dealership, I was scared to death. I was sure somebody was going to do something because the downfall of Ferrari of Los Gatos was not like a regular business going under. My Ferrari dealership was so well known, it had a ripple effect that people never stopped talking about. No one could believe that would ever happen, including me."

The aftermath of Ferrari of Los Gatos going out of business hit the headlines of major newspapers across the country. When most car dealerships went out of business, it showed up in small print in the newspaper legal notice section that nobody reads. But when the Ferrari dealership went under, it seemed like every media outlet had something to say. And people on the street couldn't believe it happened. They couldn't stop talking about it. Social media chat sites still talk about it today, some 30 years later.

The reaction might have been so strong because the dealership was known throughout the world, but it was also because the U.S. government used it to make a point about bankruptcy fraud.

Brian had no contact with Ferrari for years, but, like the sound of Jim Kimberly's V-12 engine firing up in 1954, he didn't go a day without thinking about it. He still harbored the sick feeling in the pit of his stomach that he had lost what was once the most successful Ferrari dealership in North America. Not only had he lost the dealership and everything he owned, but customers had lost as well. Some lost money, others the car of their dreams. Maybe no one lost as much as Brian, but he still felt terrible about it. He never wanted that to happen to anyone.

Living out of his change jar for a while and selling anything he could to raise money (he still had a couple of Rolex watches left), Brian tried to make a comeback.

It wasn't easy.

He had a hard time walking down the street in Los Gatos. He felt as though every person he passed turned to look at him. A voice inside his head kept repeating, *They know who you are and what happened.* While Brian had the presence of mind to realize this was absurd, managing the stress and tension it created was difficult. At times, he found it hard to breathe. *Would he ever be himself again,* he wondered?

Not wanting to be seen in Los Gatos, he and his girlfriend stopped going to local bars and restaurants where he'd spent most of the past 20 years. Instead, neighborhoods in San Jose became the place they hung out. He was pretty sure no one knew who he was at the bars and restaurants there, and they could enjoy a relaxing dinner. "I'd go to Willow Glen or Alum Rock in San Jose, somewhere that nobody knew me. I just couldn't face anybody. In my mind, I had blown up the best Ferrari dealership in the United States, and it was my fault. I was too messed up to see what was going on or to fight back."

But the statute of limitations was approaching, and Brian hoped that would end the pain and anguish over the demise of Ferrari of Los Gatos. He'd had enough of the phone calls where no one said anything and hung up and the never-ending calls from the woman at the California Department of Motor Vehicles (DMV) who seemed like she just wanted to do something bad to him. She felt he should pay for the losses caused by Ferrari of Los Gatos, especially when California sales tax and DMV fees were not paid. Even after the district attorney explained that this was a bankruptcy and that Brian was not personally liable, she continued to call. He'd suffered harassment from the DMV, customers, businesses, and employees that had lost money, and he was ready to move forward with his life. Finally, he was starting to see the light at the end of the tunnel and felt like he was starting to recover, making money once again and helping a friend at his dealership in Campbell. He lived with his girlfriend and felt happy again for the first time since he'd lost Ferrari of Los Gatos.

But enemies have a way of putting obstacles in front of you whenever you are getting close to something they don't want you to have. Unfortunately, Brian's happiness was going to be short lived. It may have been over with Ferrari, but a new antagonist was lurking in the shadows.

Every morning, Brian walked outside to get the newspaper. One morning, he noticed a white van with no windows and a small satellite dish on top. *Odd*, he thought, but dismissed it. When he saw the van there repeatedly, he decided to go find out what was going on. "I walked down the street to look inside the van. Even the front door had dark-tinted windows, so it was hard to see inside. I did notice the outline of a person sitting behind the steering wheel. As I got closer, planning to knock on the driver's window, the motor started, and the van pulled away. I didn't know it at the time, but it must have been an FBI surveillance team. For all I knew, they had been watching me for some time and may have been listening as well. *What's going on?* was all I could think."

The following Monday, Brian was brushing his teeth when he heard pounding on the front door. The next thing he knew, six FBI agents were in his living room asking if he was Brian Burnett and if he had any weapons in the house. They treated him as if he were a wanted criminal.

"You need to come with us," said the agent in charge. They escorted him outside and into a waiting vehicle.

"Where are we going?" Brian asked, sitting between two agents in the backseat.

"San Francisco."

"Why San Francisco?"

"It's a holiday weekend and there aren't any court judges on duty today. There's a magistrate up there."

Brian knew he was being arrested and asked them to handcuff him in the front and not in the back. He was thankful they complied. "The agents were nice, but I was scared. It was a long ride, and when we finally got there, we walked in together."

The magistrate looked up at the group. "Well, what are you doing here this morning?"

One of the agents handed the magistrate some papers to read. It seems the FBI was convinced Brian had taken money from Ferrari of Los Gatos and diverted it into bank accounts in Switzerland. They were reaching for anything they could to get Brian before the statute of limitations ran out.

Every year, Brian's dad took a group on what he called a "Swiss Trek." Rex had traveled there before and was familiar with exciting places to go for some fun sightseeing. One year, needing a break and change of scenery, Brian decided to join the group. He flew over with his girlfriend and met up with his dad and the rest of the group. "When we arrived in Switzerland, we went into the first bank we saw to exchange some American money into Swiss francs. That's the only thing I ever did in any Swiss bank. Somehow, the FBI knew about it and assumed I must have opened an account and deposited stolen money. It was just days before the statute of limitations ran out when they came and grabbed me."

The magistrate finished reading the paperwork, removed his glasses, and glanced up at Brian. "It looks like they woke you up, son?"

"Honestly, your honor, I don't know why they brought me here."

"Well, I read the papers they have here listing the reasons they want me to put you in jail, but for the life of me, I can't figure out why they brought you here either."

Turning to the agents, the magistrate asked, "What are you doing bringing this guy up here on this type of charge?" The agents looked at him but didn't know what to say.

In the silence, the magistrate turned to Brian and said, "Go on home, son, I need to talk to these guys."

Brian called his attorney, Mike Morrissey, who drove up to San Francisco and brought him home.

Within days, Brian was indicted for lying under oath in the petition he'd submitted to the bankruptcy court.

The allegations may have been unfounded, but Brian needed solid legal help to fight the U.S. government. His attorney, Mike Morrissey, was going through personal problems and had a suspended license, and Wayne Thomas, the lawyer he'd used to fight Ford, had a conflict of interest. "I asked around to find out who was the toughest criminal defense attorney in the area. The name Paul Meltzer kept coming up."

Meltzer set the bar for criminal defense work in Santa Cruz County. He'd been able to get sentences reduced to probation and community service in many high-profile cases. And he commanded respect from the police, prosecutors, and others he challenged in court. One longtime sheriff's deputy said, "As soon as any of us gets in trouble, we don't walk, we sprint over to his [Meltzer's] office."

Brian had found his man.

In 1996, on average, a Silicon Valley high-tech company went public every five days, creating 62 new millionaires. As a result, more than 50,000 new jobs were created, and local wages were growing at five times the national average. "This is an economic miracle taking place right before our eyes," said Thomas M. Siebel, founder of software maker Siebel Systems, Inc. His company raised $33 million going public in June 1996, grew to $1.3 billion in sales in 2004, and employed more than 5,000 people. In 2005, it was acquired by Oracle for $5.8 billion.

But not all the newly public companies fared this well. Silicon Valley bankruptcies were growing at an alarming rate, and many companies went broke. Investors were losing their money and wanted the government to fix things.

The U.S. Justice Department announced an increased prosecution effort dubbed Operation Total Disclosure. Ordered by U.S. Attorney General Janet Reno, the probe's goal was to show that illegally hiding assets, filing falsified petitions, or otherwise abusing the legal system would not be tolerated. In addition, her mission was to find bankruptcy filings that could be used to discourage others from defrauding the government.

The Silicon Valley FBI office struggled to find high-profile bankruptcy cases that would achieve Reno's goal. There were stacks and stacks of cases to review, but none of the companies involved were well known. As a result, no one would recognize the names of these bankrupt companies. They needed a poster-child company to make their point, and they couldn't find one.

Other FBI units, along with the tax and criminal divisions of the Justice Department, the Internal Revenue Service, and the Postal Inspection Service, had been able to find cases involving only real estate or small-business bankruptcies. One individual was indicted for transferring phony partnership stakes in troubled properties to a bankrupt person to stall foreclosures. Another sporting goods merchant claimed to have no remaining inventory when filing for bankruptcy but was found to have $70,000 of merchandise in his garage, car trunk, and storage locker. In Los Angeles, a defendant secretly transferred money from a troubled gas station into other accounts and did not disclose this to the bankruptcy court. And a Pennsylvania man filed to clear his debts five times in five years, each time allegedly concealing his previous difficulty. While these were clear violations and misuse of the bankruptcy system, they weren't headline news. Most people would read these articles and say, "So what, who cares?"

FBI agents told Brian that they were so dissatisfied with the cases highlighted by the San Jose investigative team that a special task force from Las Vegas was brought in. Along with agents from the IRS criminal investigation division, the Nevada FBI team sifted through pile after pile of closed bankruptcy cases for weeks. When an agent noticed the word "Ferrari" in the title of a 1994 bankruptcy filing, he jumped up. It may have occurred five years earlier, but he figured the word "Ferrari" might get the attention his superiors were after. After all, everyone on earth recognized the name Ferrari. Maybe this was the jewel they'd been searching for.

Brian remembered them telling him that when the Las Vegas agents showed the case to the other agents, excitement filled the room. The team figured if they could find anything to prosecute the individuals involved with a Ferrari dealership, they'd have accomplished their supervisor's goal. Moreover, the agents told Brian that the agency believed that by setting an example of bankruptcy fraud involving this famous car, they'd have the headline news that people would want to read.

They were right.

The government claimed Brian defrauded the public and California. They alleged he took more than one deposit on the same vehicle, diverted money into other companies he owned, and failed to report sales to the DMV.

The charges included six counts of bankruptcy fraud, including failure to report the sale of a $112,000 Ferrari during bankruptcy proceedings and other false promises regarding the delivery of new Ferraris. There may have been a clerical error regarding the unreported sale, but Brian was not personally responsible for the misstatement. Ferrari, on the other hand, was responsible for not delivering cars to Ferrari of Los Gatos.

The government may have had Brian on the ropes, but when he arrived in court with attorney Paul Meltzer, the prosecutors almost fell off their chairs. Everything changed, and the government was now ready to negotiate. With his new powerhouse defense attorney, Brian was prepared to fight.

When he asked his new attorney how they should proceed, what he heard was different than what he expected.

"Brian, they will never stop coming after you, and you cannot win. They don't stop. They have taxpayer money and can put 50 people on the case if they need to. They are like an alligator; they bite and don't let go. Let me present a plea bargain. They'll get what they're after, and you'll probably get a reduced sentence and maybe pay a small fine. I'm not sure if there will be jail time or other community service, but we can negotiate the best for you, maybe just probation. It won't end unless we do this. And remember, you don't have money to continue paying me either."

Brian asked a friend who was a judge for advice. "Brian, they would not be doing any of this to you if the word 'Ferrari' was not on the paperwork. And, because the word 'Ferrari' is on the paperwork, they will never stop until they accomplish their mission. Like your attorney told you, they have probably already spent millions coming after you, and there is no way they will quit now. They have unlimited funds. You have none."

Brian decided to take his attorney Meltzer's advice and agreed to one count of bankruptcy fraud for not reporting accurately to the bankruptcy court. The judge gave Brian a six-month sentence, probation after that, and a $24,000 fine.

He'd run a great race. The factory in Maranello had confirmed that Ferrari of Los Gatos was the number one dealer in North America during one of the trips. He had a beautiful wife and family, an incredible home, a beautiful boat, and unique cars. For a while, he had anything he wanted. But he took his eye off the ball, and all was gone in an instant.

"They put me through hell, but I never did any jail time."

To serve his six-month sentence, Brian became a part-time resident at a halfway house in Salinas, California. When he arrived and knocked on the door, they wouldn't let him in. Thinking he was either lost or crazy, the manager told him to go away. They were not used to having a guest drive up in a car wearing a polo shirt and Bermuda shorts. Brian remembered going back to his car to find the court papers to prove he was supposed to stay there.

His roommates were ex-criminals in transit from prison back to life in public. Many of them shared stories he couldn't repeat—not because they made him swear to keep them secret but because no one would believe them.

"Inmates were only allowed to leave the house when they were on a job interview, except for me. I drove to Salinas from Los Gatos every evening to arrive by eight. The others were required to stay at the house 24 hours a day. My sentence said I could work during the day but had to stay at the halfway house between 8 p.m. and 8 a.m., except for Sundays, when I had to spend 24 hours on the premises. I was the only guy with a car, and since I was out in the real world during the day, I showed up with movies, magazines, and newspapers. I got along well with everyone, no matter what group or gang they were part of. Some of the rooms were off limits, but I could go anywhere because they all liked me. I felt terrible for them and tried to show some kindness by bringing them things from the world outside. No one had been nice to them for a long time."

Brian kept a large jar next to his bed and put his pocket change in it each night. This was something he'd done most of his life. At the halfway house, the jar became the other resident's bank. They all knew where it was and enjoyed using it when necessary. A typical request went something like this.

"Brian, can I borrow a dollar to get something out of the vending machine?"

"Yeah, go ahead and get it."

"What do you mean?"

"Go ahead and get it. Just take a dollar, and when you can, pay me back."

Brian trusted his fellow residents, and they were not used to that. He was teaching them something that wasn't in the official rehabilitation program. Sometimes, unplanned or unrehearsed lessons can be the most valuable.

"It was amazing. During the entire time I was there, no one took money without asking, and everyone made sure I knew they paid me back. These ex-criminals showed me better ethics than most businessmen I had dealt with during Ferrari of Los Gatos. And some of them shared their escapades with me."

THE PIZZA BANDIT

In 1987, Ron Howell, known as the Pizza Parlor Bandit, broke out of the Santa Cruz County Jail with Murl Craig, the so-called Budweiser

Bandit. Ron received his nickname because he liked to rob pizza parlors. His trademark was taking a pizza with the cash. His escape partner, Murl Craig, robbed grocery stores and was known as the Budweiser Bandit because he always approached the grocery store clerk carrying a six-pack of Budweiser beer. Beer and pizza go together, so it makes perfect sense the two would try and escape at the same time.

They planned to saw through steel security bars and crawl into a room with a glass window. Once inside, they'd use the steel bars to smash the window and get to freedom. The biggest challenge they faced was Ron's weight. He couldn't fit through the crawl space into the adjoining room—probably because of too many pizzas. So Ron was allowed to eat only salads and vegetables until he could fit. In the meantime, the meat, bread, and potatoes went to Murl and two other inmates.

They used a string, coated with toothpaste and cleanser, to saw through the bars. Their plan was clever and worked, but their freedom didn't last long.

After robbing a pizza parlor in Santa Barbara, the Pizza Bandit was arrested in Southern California. The Budweiser Bandit was captured in Walnut Creek a couple of nights later. Both ended up back in the county jail within a week.

THE BANK ROBBER

One of Brian's roommates was a successful bank robber. Well, successful 39 out of 40 times. He'd been robbing banks in the United States for years without getting caught. He told Brian, "Once I'd accumulated enough money to live comfortably, I split to Mexico." While he enjoyed a luxurious lifestyle there, he missed the sense of adventure bank robbing had provided. He decided on one more adrenaline rush in the United States; then, he'd stop and live in Mexico for good.

He planned to carry out the job the same way he had in the past. "I didn't want to fix what wasn't broken." But he needed someone to help him with the getaway car. The only person he could trust was an old girl-friend. She agreed to drive the car, and he gave her clear instructions on where and when to pick him up.

On the day of the robbery, he came out of the bank, and there was no transportation waiting for him. She swore it was because she got scared, had a panic attack, and drove down the wrong street. He told Brian he never knew for sure what went wrong. But he had left her when he went to Mexico—maybe she was unhappy about that.

Brian enjoyed the others he met at the halfway house and felt good bringing them magazines, newspapers, and videos from the outside. The six months went by fast, and he remembered the day he was checking out of the halfway house for the last time. "I visited the other residents, said good-bye, and wished them good luck. When I reached the front door, I looked up at the halfway house manager—he had tears in his eyes. I shook his hand as he told me, 'We're losing our spark plug. You energized this place every night, and the residents' attitudes improved when you were here. You've had a more positive effect on this place than anyone ever did.'"

In that manager's eyes, Brian had become number one again.

Back in the real world, there were still 300 hours of community service to complete to satisfy his sentence. So, he went to work doing what he did best. Brian looked for older cars in driveways and garages in the community and asked the owners to donate them to Los Gatos High School. He discovered many of the residents had children at the school or had attended it themselves and used that leverage to convince them to donate their car. He then sold the car for top dollar, and the proceeds went to the school. Brian raised a total of $170,000 and more than fulfilled the court's order of 300 hours. The high school couldn't believe what Brian had accomplished and to show their appreciation dedicated a park bench on the school campus to him.

The day he received the court notice that he had fulfilled his obligations and the case against him and Ferrari of Los Gatos was closed, he sat on that bench. Reflecting that maybe his ordeal was finally over, he glanced down East Main Street. Two blocks away, he could see a sign that said Silicon Valley Auto Group hanging where the word "Ferrari" and the prancing horse logo used to be. He looked down the street in the opposite direction and saw the Los Gatos library parking lot where he hung out as a teenager.

In his mind, he could hear and see the customers, employees, and others associated with the dealership once again. He realized he had spent most of the last 43 years of his life in this two-block radius. He'd gone to school here, sold cars in the library parking lot, and grown a small street corner car lot into the country's most lucrative and well-known Ferrari dealership.

He remembered the day he'd left the dealership and locked the door for the last time, and he wondered once more, *What now, what next?*

Epilogue

The Next 20 Years

THEY MAY HAVE TAKEN HIS DEALERSHIP BUT NOT HIS PASSION FOR CARS. That's in his blood and will be if there's a breath in his body. Brian continues to locate hard-to-find classic cars, and he does it the same way he did in the 1980s—over the phone.

During the Ferrari of Los Gatos years, Brian developed relationships with many wealthy individuals who loved cars. Today, he's always on the hunt for the next deal, and when he finds one now, all he needs to do is phone a friend.

Sometimes, a friend phones him.

"Hey Brian, I've found some Ferraris in a storage shed. An attorney representing the owner says they've been there for years, and I can go over and look at them. Do you think you could find a buyer for them?"

"Hell, yeah!"

Brian had met Wayne Davis many years earlier. The two bonded over a few car deals and became good buddies. Even after Ferrari of Los Gatos was gone, the two remained friends and continue to do business together.

"Wayne called me in the 1980s about one of the ultimate muscle cars of all time, a Pontiac Super Duty 421, and I went to his home in Texas to see it. That was the first of many deals we did over the years, and it was the start of a darn good friendship. I can't begin to add up all the Ferraris, Porsches, Maseratis, and muscle cars that went through our hands."

In 2011, after phoning Brian, Wayne went to see the cars in the storage shed. He took pictures and sent them to Brian, who promptly called him back.

"What's the story on these cars, Wayne?"

"Well, the attorney representing the owner called Wayne Carini, the popular host of the reality television program *Chasing Classic Cars*. He said he'd seen him on TV and didn't know who else to call. It sounds like Carini's already seen them and made an offer."

"How much do you think he offered?" asked Brian.

"I think he offered $500,000."

Brian knew what the cars were worth even though he couldn't see them under the inches of dust.

"Offer $550,000 and don't let 'em get away."

When a classic car is discovered after being stored, it's called a "barn find." The term comes from the long history of great finds in barns, sheds, or other unassuming buildings after being stored for years. A barn find usually applies to rare and valuable vehicles, the ones that even in poor condition are of interest to collectors and enthusiasts.

Some barn finds command high prices when sold. For example, a 1967 Ferrari 330 GTS Spyder brought in $2.1 million in January 2014. The car had suffered an engine fire in 1969 and remained in a garage for 44 years. Despite its damaged condition, it sold for more than what a fully restored model brought a year before. Restorations sometimes lower

2011 barn find: '72 Ferrari Daytona, '73 Ferrari Dino, '77 Maserati Bora.
Personal photo Brian Burnett

the value of a car. There's something about leaving a treasure the way it's discovered. It preserves the evidence surrounding its history.

Wayne drove to the attorney's office, went in without an appointment, and made a deal for $550,000. They decided not to do anything to the cars, not even wash them. Brian just did what he did best—he got on the phone and found someone interested in the cars. He called his friend Terry Price. Terry had worked at Ferrari of Los Gatos for many years and continued buying and selling classic cars after the dealership closed.

When Brian was moving to South Carolina, he decided to visit Terry on the way. "I was ready for a break from the California craziness. So I decided to head back to the Southeast, where I'd spent much of my childhood. On the way, I stopped to see Terry and ended up spending the winter in his guesthouse. During those four months, I helped him with his business, including when he sold the barn find cars a second time."

The three cars were a '72 Ferrari 365 GTB/4 Daytona (9,752 miles), a '73 Ferrari Dino 246 GTS (2,910 miles), and a '77 Maserati Bora Coupe (978 miles). The owner of the cars was Howard O'Flynn, a banker from New York and one of Enzo's first U.S. clients.

The cars were posted on eBay with Wayne's pictures, dust and all. The auto website bringatrailer.com picked up the listing as well. This site allowed people to share comments and opinions about car deals. Most listings got some comments, but Brian's barn find story set a record—268 comments, most of them in the first two days.

Readers could not believe that a serious eBay listing would show pictures of cars covered with so much dust. They made comments like "Someone put a bag of dust in a shop vac and blew it on the cars after staging them" or "How come I don't see any footprints." One reader claimed, "The Bora dust is simply too flawless to be real."

Most of the comments suggested that the listing had to be a scam and that that's why they didn't clean up the cars. Buyer beware, they warned, the seller doesn't want you to see what's under that blanket of dust.

It was marketing genius. As the record-setting comments rolled in over the internet, Brian received a phone call from an advertising executive at Mecum Auctions, the world leader in collector and classic car live auctions. The Mecum Auction Company started in 1988 with a few friends around Dana Mecum's dining room table, planning its first auction at the Rockford, Illinois, airport. Today the company is ranked the number one world leader of collector cars offered at auction, collector cars sold at auction, number of auction venues, and total dollar volume of sales. It is host to the world's largest collector car auction held annually in Kissimmee, Florida. They also run the world's largest motorcycle auction held annually in Las Vegas.

The Mecum advertising executive was interested in finding out more about the barn find and asked if the cars were still available. Brian told him, "You can't buy those cars and make any money on 'em." He was told that Dana didn't want to make money reselling them; he wanted them for advertising. After all, this was one of the most talked-about barn finds in history. Brian helped Terry sell the cars for a second time, and Mecum ran them through the 2011 Monterey auction. Mecum lost money on them but said they drew a lot of attention.

While the storage shed find was exciting, Brian made his favorite discovery on a farm in Indiana.

George, a truck driver who had handled many muscle car deals with Brian, was taking a driving break at a farm equipment estate sale. After looking at dozens of John Deere tractors, combines, and row crop headers, George got bored and decided to get back on the road. As he walked past the house, he happened to glance through the window of the garage door. What he saw startled him. He couldn't believe his eyes. Parked in the garage was a Lamborghini Miura SV, a Ferrari Daytona, a Lamborghini Espada, a Dodge Viper Coupe, and a Jaguar XK120 roadster. He called Brian immediately to tell him what he'd found.

"Screw the tractors," Brian told him. "Go to the attorney or whoever's in charge, stay away from the auctioneers, and find out how much they want for the cars."

Next, Brian called his friend Wayne, who agreed to buy them. They got all five cars for $775,000.

One of the cars, the Miura SV, was worth almost that much alone. In 1971, Lamborghini introduced the car in Geneva as "the world's first supercar." The Miura SV (the "V" stands for "veloce," or superfast) was hands down the best Miura version ever produced at the time. In 1973, after building only 150, Lamborghini took the car out of production. It became super valuable to go along with superfast. Many car collectors call it the most beautiful car ever produced in series.

The Lamborghini sold for $700,000, which set a world record at the time. It almost paid for everything, so Brian and Wayne gave the Dodge Viper to George for locating the cars. That made him very happy.

Technically, this wasn't a barn find, but from a financial standpoint, it was the best find either had ever come across.

As I write this epilogue, two of Brian's Georgia buddies have come across a pair of 1966 Jaguar E-Type Coupes in a small town about 90 miles outside Atlanta. He didn't hesitate to tell them he'll have someone interested in them soon.

"I can't stop looking for cars. Part of the fun is the hunt."

After 20 years, a friend asked Brian to help locate high-quality vehicles for his classic car dealership. His friend's lot and showroom are not far from where Brian got his start, and although he's a resident of South Carolina now, Brian's back doing what he did in the 1960s. Things haven't changed. A long time ago, he learned it's easier to become number one when you're not like everyone else. And today, Brian's still locating classic cars and making deals.

Brian was at the friend's dealership recently and stood on the showroom floor looking at a 1966 Chevrolet Corvette Sting Ray 427 Roadster, a 1936 Ford Deluxe Phaeton, and a 1951 Cadillac Series 62 Convertible. It brought back memories.

One of the young employees struggled to start the Ford Phaeton. He glanced over at Brian.

Brian smiled. "Just pull the choke out a little bit and tap the gas pedal, but only once," he said. "After she starts up, use the gas pedal to keep her running."

No, things haven't changed. And for Brian they probably never will.

ACKNOWLEDGMENTS

BEHIND EVERY BOOK IS MORE THAN JUST AN AUTHOR. THERE'S A TEAM, a support group, family, and friends. And as most authors know, writing a book is a long journey, and to finish, you need every one of these people to motivate you. You also need a passion inside your soul to overcome hurdles and help you continue when your mind says you can't do anymore. My passion started with a flashlight.

Mom would turn out the light, whisper, "Now get to sleep," and close the door on her way out. When I couldn't hear her footsteps anymore, the sheets went over my head, and the flashlight clicked on. It was usually an episode of *The Hardy Boys Mystery Stories*, but I believe my love of writing started with reading. I also remember two things on my dad's nightstand when he went to bed: Vicks VapoRub and a copy of *Reader's Digest*. Thanks, Dad, for setting an example that reading was important.

Fast-forward many years, and I have many to thank. Of course, my schoolteachers must come first. I can't remember all their names, but a few are etched in my mind. Mrs. Bradshaw, English (a subject I did not enjoy); Jim McCavitt, elementary school (he taught me the importance of research and being aware of current events); John Ziegler, California State University, Chico, accounting professor (more than a teacher, he was a dear friend who called me a young man in such a hurry and told me I could accomplish anything I set my mind to); and Keith Ekiss, Stanford University professor (his creative nonfiction class got me started, and his suggestions helped direct my writing path).

Today, I can locate only one college schoolbook on my bookshelf. It's titled *Communicating through Letters and Reports* by J. H. Menning and C. W. Wilkinson. I never met them, but their book must have influenced my writing—almost every page contains underlined words and my hand-written notes in the margin.

More recently, several people helped produce *The Dealer*. Stewart Griffith, my consultant, Web administrator, and creator of www.FLGstory.com. Thank you for teaching me how to use WordPress and then always being there to fix what I screwed up. Helga Schier, my editor who not only helped my words tell the story better but motivated me when she said, "I don't know anything about cars, but I like the way you tell the story." Thank you, Helga; your comment gave me the perseverance to carry on when obstacles or other opinions got in the way. Bob Pimm, my literary attorney who helped me navigate the business of being an author. I'm so glad you were able to put legal terms in layman's language for me. And every author needs a good partner in a literary agent, and I was lucky to snag one of the best. It took me more than 400 days to find Anne Devlin of the Max Gartenberg Agency, and it took her only 40 days to get a publisher interested. Thank you for continuing the passion your father started many years ago and thank you for believing in *The Dealer*.

And most importantly, my writing coach, Nina Amir. I know this book and myriad things that support it could not have been done without you. You recommended most of the team to me, taught me how to blog my book, and helped me craft a book proposal that worked. Your valuable advice, motivational phone calls, and pushing me to get things done helped *The Dealer* cross the finish line. I will be forever grateful.

It's entirely possible that Bill Glau, one of the first friends I met when I moved to Los Gatos, is the one responsible for this book. One night, while having dinner with him at Forbes Mill Steakhouse, he set things in motion when he said, "Jim, this is my friend Brian Burnett. He used to own Ferrari of Los Gatos." None of us knew what the future would hold, but in one way or another, *The Dealer* probably started that night. Thank you, Bill, for your friendship and the introduction.

To my daughters Lia and Kim, you motivated me to continue when you said how proud of me you were for writing this book.

And thank you, Corinne, for believing in me and giving me the space and time needed to complete this book. Without your love and support, I could not have done it.

A special thank-you to Brian's family, friends, employees, and a few enemies for sharing their part of the 20-year ride. You helped me gain a better understanding of what it must have been like being part of Ferrari of Los Gatos.

And, lastly, to my friend Brian Burnett for sharing many hours with me telling the story. You allowed me to write while you struggled through the pain of recalling some memories you'd been trying to forget. I thank you for the opportunity and for helping me achieve my goal to become an author.